# Deepening the Leadership Journey

*Deepening the Leadership Journey* is a compendium of topical (and in some cases imponderable) situations for which leadership is either applicable or in need.

This new book uses the nine elements in application to five challenges facing the current generation of leaders: making good decisions in an increasingly complex world; motivating and retaining a qualified workforce; equality and a truly diverse and inclusive workplace; cultivating a positive organizational culture; and thriving in a digital world.

Intended for personal leadership development and practicing managers as well as courses on leadership, this approachable guide deepens the reader's leadership journey based on Al Bolea's "J-Curve" model of leadership and the nine essential elements of leadership mastery introduced in *Becoming a Leader*.

**Al Bolea** is the founder and architect of the Applied Leadership Seminars, the former CEO/GM of a large independent oil company in the United Arab Emirates, and a retired executive from a major international oil and gas company, as well as former Distinguished Visiting Professor of Leadership at the University of Alaska and a Guest Leadership Lecturer at the University of Houston.

**Leanne Atwater** is the C.T. Bauer Professor of Leadership and Management in the Bauer College of Business at the University of Houston. She teaches leadership development and conducts executive education classes. She is also a former editor of *The Leadership Quarterly*.

# Leadership: Research and Practice Series

**Series Editor**

**Ronald E. Riggio**, Henry R. Kravis Professor of Leadership and Organizational Psychology and former Director of the Kravis Leadership Institute at Claremont McKenna College.

*In Memoriam*
*Georgia Sorenson (1947–2020)*

**Leadership and the Ethics of Influence**
*Terry L. Price*

**When Leaders Face Personal Crisis: The Human Side of Leadership**
*Gill Robinson Hickman and Laura E. Knouse*

**Inclusive Leadership: Transforming Diverse Lives, Workplaces, and Societies**
*Edited by Bernardo M. Ferdman, Jeanine Prime, and Ronald E. Riggio*

**Becoming a Leader: Nine Elements of Leadership Mastery**
*Al Bolea and Leanne Atwater*

**Leadership Across Boundaries: A Passage to Aporia**
*Nathan Harter*

**A Theory of Environmental Leadership: Leading for the Earth**
*Mark Manolopoulos*

**Handbook of International and Cross-Cultural Leadership Research Processes: Perspectives, Practice, Instruction**
*Edited by Yulia Tolstikov-Mast, Franziska Bieri, and Jennie L. Walker*

For more information about this series, please visit:
www.routledge.com/Leadership-Research-and-Practice/book-series/leadership

# Deepening the Leadership Journey

## NINE ELEMENTS OF LEADERSHIP MASTERY

Al Bolea
and Leanne Atwater

Routledge
Taylor & Francis Group

NEW YORK AND LONDON

Cover image: © Shutterstock

First published 2022
by Routledge
605 Third Avenue, New York, NY 10158

and by Routledge
2 Park Square, Milton Park, Abingdon, Oxon, OX14 4RN

*Routledge is an imprint of the Taylor & Francis Group, an informa business*

*Library of Congress Cataloging-in-Publication Data*
Names: Bolea, Al, author. | Atwater, Leanne E., author.
Title: Deepening the leadership journey : nine elements of leadership
    mastery / Al Bolea and Leanne Atwater.
Description: New York, NY : Routledge, 2022. | Series: Leadership—
    research and practice | Includes bibliographical references
    and index.
Identifiers: LCCN 2021032744 (print) | LCCN 2021032745 (ebook) |
    ISBN 9780367478377 (hardback) | ISBN 9780367478360 (paperback) |
    ISBN 9781003036791 (ebook)
Subjects: LCSH: Leadership. | Management. | Decision making. |
    Corporate culture. | Executive ability.
Classification: LCC HD57.7 .B6386 2022 (print) | LCC HD57.7 (ebook) |
    DDC 658.4/092—dc23
LC record available at https://lccn.loc.gov/2021032744
LC ebook record available at https://lccn.loc.gov/2021032745

ISBN: 978-0-367-47837-7 (hbk)
ISBN: 978-0-367-47836-0 (pbk)
ISBN: 978-1-003-03679-1 (ebk)

DOI: 10.4324/9781003036791

Typeset in Palatino
by Apex CoVantage, LLC

*Al: to Leah, Olivia, and Ben – extending my leadership journey to new generations.*

*Leanne:  to my grandchildren, Jason, Zachary, Elena, Mateo, Daniel, Sadie and Ellie who bring me pride, joy, and laughter.*

# CONTENTS

# SERIES FOREWORD

One of the greatest mistakes a leader can make is believing that they know it all, or at least that they have mastered leadership. Truly great leaders understand that they must continue to develop their leadership competencies – that they can always get better.

There are many strategies that leaders can use to continuously improve their ability to lead. Courses, workshops, and certificate programs, offered by university business schools, or leader development organizations, are a common path. Mentoring programs are another avenue for development. Gaining popularity every year is the use of leadership coaches. These leadership development programs, along with a lot of dedication and hard work, are what make good leaders into great leaders.

Which brings us to this book. It is the second volume in a series by these two fine authors, and the goal of both books is to help build leadership in new, and not so new, leaders. In the first book, *Becoming a Leader*, Al Bolea and Leanne Atwater, serve as "virtual" coaches to both aspiring and accomplished leaders. It is a wonderful and inspired combination to have an accomplished leader (Bolea), and an established academic scholar (Atwater) as your coach–guides. Using their Nine Elements of Leadership Mastery (NELM) model as a framework, they offer scientifically grounded, but practical, advice for improving leadership. (I challenge you to come up with a leadership dilemma that is not addressed in these books!)

In this new book, *Deepening the Leadership Journey*, Bolea and Atwater continue the coaching and development of their reader/leaders. With their many decades of experience in leadership research and practice, the authors present the many and complex situations that leaders face, and offer advice for dealing with each. There is such a wealth of leadership knowledge and strategy in both of these books that either one alone can be a priceless leader development program. But, together, *Becoming a Leader* and *Deepening the Leadership Journey*, is a master course in exemplary leadership development.

# ABOUT THE AUTHORS

The co-authors have written three leadership books together. They came to the leadership field from entirely different directions.

**Al Bolea** was a college dropout until his future was changed by the chance encounter with a mentor and leader as a young adult. Eventually, he earned undergraduate and graduate degrees in business. Early in his career he worked closely with many CEO- and chairman-level executives in the oil and gas industry. He went on to be a senior executive in the same industry and worked in the US, the UK, and United Arab Emirates. Much of what he writes about in the book comes from the good and bad leadership qualities of these individuals, amplified by his experiences as a leader, business executive, and leadership trainer. These experiences were further shaped through training and interactions with theorists and practitioners in the field of leadership. Al is a former Distinguished Visiting Professor of Leadership at the University of Alaska, a guest lecturer at the University of Houston, and he is the founder and owner of a leadership training company, Applied Leadership Seminars.

**Leanne Atwater** was a straight A student who went from high school through graduate school, ultimately earning a PhD in Psychology while working full time. She worked for the US Navy as a civilian Personnel Research Psychologist and was a Professor of Leadership and Psychology at the US Naval Academy. Her interest in leadership began early in her career, while studying military leaders at all levels. At age 36, she was offered (and accepted) a job to become a tenure-track professor at Binghamton University. At Binghamton she had the opportunity to work with some of the most prominent leadership researchers in the world. She has continued to study leadership throughout her career, and also consults and conducts leadership training. She spent 11 years in various academic leadership positions including Interim Dean of the School of Global Management and Leadership at Arizona State University. She is currently a Professor of Leadership at the University of Houston C.T. Bauer College of Business.

Al and Leanne met late in life and have become good friends and colleagues. They do not agree on everything when it comes to leadership and have argued about some of the details in the book – but they do agree that leadership is the essential driver of potential in people and organizations.

# PRELUDE

We, Al and Leanne, wrote our first book together in 2015. That book, *Applied Leadership Development*, is not about leadership; it is about how to lead. It provides a set of tools for anyone in any situation to become their best at leading others and organizations. Our primary audience for the book was students enrolled in university programs. However, we discovered that the book had equal appeal to readers in the workforce who were interested in personal and career development.

When our publisher approached us in 2019 about writing a revision, we wanted the new book to have more content for personal development and we even changed the title to *Becoming a Leader*. While writing the revision, we discovered that we had too much new content, and the book would exceed the publisher's guidelines for word count and page length. That is when we decided to write a third book, *Deepening the Leadership Journey*.

While our first two books provided a leadership *tool kit*, this book illustrates the application of the tools. It is a compendium of topical (and in some cases imponderable) situations for which leadership is either applicable or in need. We take deep dives into the following:

- Godliness vs. Machiavellianism – Does either reflect leadership?
- Making quality decisions in uncertain and shifting environments
- Creating and sustaining a motivated workforce – we call this "The Glow"
- Resolving inequality – which we call "Breaking the 4th Wall"
- Creating and sustaining a healthy organizational culture
- Sustaining viability in the rapidly changing digital world.

As an added bonus we have included a chapter at the beginning of the book – "Back to the Future" – in which we refresh for readers our Nine Elements of Leadership Mastery. We have also included for each Element highlights of improvement actions that we have used to coach clients over the years to address feedback from bosses, peers, and direct reports. You will find the improvement actions to be a valuable resource.

We believe that reading *Becoming a Leader* and *Deepening the Leadership Journey* together provides a comprehensive and compelling perspective about leadership as well as examples of real world applications.

# ACKNOWLEDGMENTS

Just like it takes a community to raise a child, it takes a community to write a book. We were fortunate to have the support of our spouses, Celeste and David, who kept us sane during the "gestation" of this book.

We also owe a debt of gratitude to the many colleagues who were either interviewed for the book or reviewed various chapters and gave us helpful feedback. These include Tyler Andrews, Patty Beach, John Burns, Scott Burton, Diane Decker, John Denny, Grant Kelly, Rachel Morris, Greg Riedel, Molly Ridout, Angela Rodell, and Terry Schurtleff.

We also would like to thank Galen Snyder, a *digital native* and PhD student at the University of Houston, for all of his research about digital transformation. We, two *digital immigrants*, could have never put this chapter together without his help. (If you do not know what *digital natives* and *immigrants* are, then you will surely enjoy Chapter 7).

# 1 BACK TO THE FUTURE

"What comes next?" is a song from the Broadway musical *Hamilton* performed by Jonathon Groff who portrays King George III.[1] The lyricist is Lin-Manuel Miranda. The song occurs in Act 1 after the Continental army defeats the British forces at Yorktown. It is meant to convey King George's belief that the revolutionaries will not be able to lead now that they are on their own – that they do not understand how difficult life is when they have to make all of the decisions and be accountable.

The performance is a farce that successfully entertains the audience through a highly exaggerated and extravagant scene. That said, there are words of wisdom about leadership nestled in Lin-Manuel's lyrics. For example, it really is hard to be a leader – it is hard to get there, and it is even harder to stay there. Leaders often feel that they are on their own and struggle with the burden of making quality decisions. The pathway is punctuated with vagaries, uncertainties, and hidden information within which successes and failures occur. When the latter is dominant, it is not uncommon to feel abandoned by those who were previously sponsors. In these situations, it can be difficult to find anyone to turn to for help. In the case of CEOs, for example, we often see them run past their sell-by date, lacking internal and external support, and with no other option than to exit the organization. The same occurs with others at lower levels in an organization, albeit with less publicity, and often not by their choice.

Bottom line from Lin-Manuel's King George: leadership is hard to achieve and sustain, but it is even harder to regain – and it takes some life experiences to understand that. This conclusion is reminiscent of the J-Curve (and the Dunning-Kruger Effect[2]) that we introduced in our first book, *Applied Leadership Development*, and expanded in its revision, *Becoming a Leader*. As illustrated in Figure 1.1, there is a tendency for people to overestimate their leadership abilities. We have observed in our practices that this confidence declines as a person learns more about leadership, and ultimately reverses towards improvement once they accumulate sufficient skills.

## REFRESHING THE NINE ELEMENTS OF LEADERSHIP MASTERY

With that in mind, we felt that it is important to refresh the Nine Elements of Leadership Mastery (NELM) that we developed in our books. In addition,

**Figure 1.1** J-Curve and Dunning-Kruger Effect

with combined experience of over 40 years between us of teaching and coaching leadership, we wanted to share some common issues clients have confronted and actions they have taken to improve their leadership.

NELM is a unique integration of 21 organizational and 22 personal leadership competencies that enhance the achievement and durability of a person's leadership. Each Element and its key competencies is summarized below along with highlights of improvement actions that we have coached clients to undertake over the years to address feedback received from bosses, peers, and direct reports. These summaries and actions can be explored more in depth by referring to *Becoming a Leader*.

There are 65 improvement actions detailed below which, as a collective, impart the shared energy of many who are in pursuit of great leadership. As you read the actions it is helpful to reflect on your own experiences.

## Five Elements of Organizational Leadership Competency

### *1. Set Direction*

We often hear someone say, or think to ourselves, "God, please show me the way." Typically, this occurs when we struggle with a tough decision. Some people encounter leaders in their life who help them make these decisions; others turn to divine inspiration. Setting direction for people and organizations is the highest priority for leaders because it meets a basic human need to have purpose and to be on a journey. The critical points in setting direction include: the act of asking questions of ourselves and others to open the door for an evolving reality; respecting one's intuition because it tends to be correct more often than chance would predict; and assimilating one's own observations with those of others in order to have a clear picture of the organization's internal and external environments. A direction becomes deliverable when risks are identified and managed, and objectives are realistic relative to the organization's capacity. A leader's messages bring a direction to life and animate it so people can see it, hear it, and feel it.

### Key Competencies

- Interrogate Reality
- Intuition
- Environmental Relationships
- Proactively Manage Risks
- Manage Spin

### Common Issues and Suggested Improvement Actions

- *Your behavior does not inspire others to trust you.* Trust is related directly to integrity, but there is also something about authenticity. To borrow from the Yiddish, a leader needs to practice being a "mensch" or as it is also referred to, "wholehearted." Always show up as the person you are, rather than the one you think everyone would like, and be willing to listen, learn, and evolve. We suggest four actions: (1) become keenly self-aware by observing how you feel in different situations, (2) find genuine connections by seeking to truly understand the people around you, (3) don't try to be perfect or act perfectly – embrace your imperfection and allow yourself to be vulnerable, and (4) get out of your head, into conversations, and allow yourself to be totally present – master the art of presence. Shutting down the self-narrative (those thoughts and sensations going on all of the time in our heads that interfere with being totally present in the situation) is perhaps the most effective way to ensure authenticity.
- *Your personal presence is weak.* It is likely that you do not talk enough relative to what people think you have to offer. This means that you might be spending too much time in your head or with self-doubts. You must push yourself to talk to people more often. A good way into this is to ask questions. And, don't compare yourself to others who you think have more to offer than you – use yourself as your benchmark (e.g., I'm doing more than I did last month). It is going to take practice. To change, you must experience the behavior that you want in order for it to become automatic, i.e., you must push yourself to have conversations with people more often.
- *Your personal influence is weak.* Increasing your influence in an organization is all about relationships. Specifically, increase your relationships outside of your specific area of responsibility. The solution is easy – have more conversations with people outside of your function or area. Make sure these are exchanges of views rather than a one-way "versation."[3] This could start with casual conversations that eventually evolve into

you being drawn into more corporate-wide issues. A good practice is to target having one conversation each day about anything with a person you don't work with. Do this for two weeks and assess your progress.

- *There's a concern about arrogance.* Humility is a hard nut to crack, especially in a culture that encourages competition and individuality. The best course of action is to be more considerate in conversations. Tactically, you would do this with the following seven steps: (1) from time to time admit that you're not the best at everything – or anything, (2) acknowledge your own faults, (3) express gratefulness for what you have, (4) don't be afraid to make mistakes, (5) admit your mistakes, (6) avoid bragging, and (7) share the credit generously.

- *You are poor at handling situations when people disagree with you, particularly in meetings.* Preempt disagreements by asking people how they feel about the goals and objectives you have identified. Be open for challenge and thank people for their feedback. But, never walk away from a disagreement – keep the conversation alive until a common ground is found. If a dispute emerges, use a confrontation technique that we learned from Susan Scott's *Fierce Conversations*[3] (We call it a Veritas Conversation): (1) confront the person involved by naming the issue that best describes what's causing you grief, (2) give an example that illustrates the issue, (3) describe how you feel about the situation, (4) clarify what's at stake if it's not resolved, (5) acknowledge your contribution to the problem and apologize if appropriate, (6) express your desire to resolve it, and (7) ask the person to respond – be silent and listen. It is described in more detail in Element 2 of *Becoming a Leader*.

- *You are suppressing your intuition in decision-making.* To shift the balance of intuition, you first need to give yourself permission to listen to it. Sounds easy, but it is not in most business situations. Technical solutions tend to dominate decision-making, which means that data and objectivity are the main inputs. The issue is that some challenges require adaptive rather than technical solutions. Without intuition, you will miss the need for adaptive changes.

- *Your values are not clear and consistent.* To get some traction with the core values issue, we suggest that you complete what we call the "What Do I Stand For" exercise. You do this by first asking yourself what you seriously value. Phrase the question like this, "What do I consider good, important, useful, desirable, or constructive?" List out words that describe each of these distinctions. Then, reach out to people who know you well and ask, "What do I stand for?" The last step is to look for a match between what you value and what others think you stand for. If there isn't a match then you need to start over again with the first question, because you have just received some evidence that what you think you value is not consistent with your behavior. The exercise will help you identify what you truly value and push you to find the courage to confront situations that conflict with these values.

- *You spend too much time focused on the past.* During every conversation that you have, find a moment to insert something that is future oriented.

People who are past driven in conversations tend to spend too much time finding problems rather than discovering new possibilities. An easy way into this is to start talking about risks – it immediately takes you into consideration of things that could happen in the future. Another idea is to intentionally try to co-create with another person a new insight or something that could emerge in the future – do this at least once each day.

- *You do not impart passion and motivation to others about the future.* Crank up your passion at work. Start by faking it, i.e., act "as if" you are passionate. Nurturing passion in the workplace is about creating and articulating a compelling future for the organization. But it also has a lot to do with "scratching the itch" of what motivates people as individuals. For each of the people with whom you have significant work relationships (including your boss), see if you can assess their relative need for the following key motivators: status, certainty, autonomy, relatedness, and fairness. (For an assessment of these motivators, complete a SCARF assessment at https://neuroleadership.com/research/tools/nli-scarf-assessment/.) Consider what you can do to meet the dominant need that you perceive for each of them.

### 2. Build a Team of People

Leaders are critical for maximizing the human capital of the organization. One of their primary tasks is to build and nurture teams. They recognize the importance of diversity in thoughts and perspectives, and they realize that the only way to understand others is to first understand oneself. (See Box 1.1 Self-Understanding and Self-Knowledge). Leaders nurture high-performing teams into existence through conversations that enable psychological safety, a condition in which team members feel included, safe to contribute, and safe to challenge the status quo without fear of being embarrassed, marginalized, or punished in some way.[4] They never ignore a conflict. Leaders realize that not confronting an issue will cause it to spread and perpetuate.

### Key Competencies

- Build Diverse Teams
- Psychological Safety
- Nurture Esprit Teams

## Box 1.1:  Self-Understanding and Self-Knowledge

Being an excellent leader includes self-understanding and self-knowledge. These are not always easy to accomplish but are worth pursuing.[5]

There are many benefits of self-knowledge. Among them are:

- You will be happier.
- You will experience less inner conflict.

- You will be able to engage in greater self-control when you understand your habits and triggers.
- You will experience less inner conflict because when you act in accordance with your values your decisions are easier.
- Your awareness of your own weaknesses will allow you to be more able to empathize with others.
- Being in touch with who you truly are helps you experience life in a more exciting and enriching way.

There are many tools you can use to understand yourself better. A few that stand out are:[5,6,7]

- Journal ... spend 10 minutes each day writing anything that comes to mind. Once a week read what you have written.
- Write down what you love and what you love to do.
- Think and write about your values. Research shows that thinking or writing about your values can make it more likely that you will make healthy choices.
- Check out some free online personality inventories.
- Ask for feedback from others about what they see as your strengths and weaknesses.
- Ask yourself: what have been the most meaningful events in your life? This may reveal clues to your hidden self.

## Box 1.2: Implicit Bias

Implicit bias refers to the attitudes or stereotypes that affect our understanding, actions, and decisions in an unconscious manner. These biases, which encompass both favorable and unfavorable assessments, are activated involuntarily and without an individual's awareness or intentional control.[8]

- Implicit biases are pervasive. Everyone possesses them, even people with avowed commitments to impartiality such as judges.
- The implicit biases we hold do not always align with what we proclaim to believe or with our sense of self or social identity.
- We generally tend to hold implicit biases that favor those similar to us.
- The good news is that implicit biases are malleable and through a variety of techniques we can learn to overcome them.[6] Being aware of the potential impact of implicit social biases allows you to take an active role in overcoming these social stereotypes and potential discrimination.[9]

One example of implicit bias has to do with ageism. While research largely shows no performance differences between older and younger employees and, in some contexts, older workers even outperform younger employees, many individuals hold implicit biases that influence their attitudes and behaviors toward older workers. Malinen and Johnston for example found that while participants in their studies reported no explicit ageist attitudes, negative, stable implicit attitudes towards older workers emerged. They suggested the importance of assessing one's implicit biases with tests such as the Harvard Implicit Attitudes Test.[10] This test allows takers to assess a variety of implicit biases toward other races, religions etc. While there are some concerns about the reliability of the test, it is eye-opening to most. (Take the test at https://implicit. harvard.edu/implicit/takeatest.html).

The conclusion is that we all have implicit biases that influence our attitudes and behaviors. The more aware we are of these biases the more likely we can consciously try to keep them from leading us to make biased decisions.

### Common Issues and Suggested Improvement Actions

- *You have favorites at work.* Address this issue through some introspection. Complete a Myers-Briggs Type Inventory (MBTI) online at www.themy-ersbriggs.com. Understand your own preferences to understand others. View each person as unique and see the potential in them. Be critically aware that you are probably labeling people, which impairs your ability to see their unique qualities. You might be unwittingly shutting down the very relationships that you need in your personal and work life. (See Box 1.2 Implicit Bias)
- *Cliques are tolerated in the organization.* The problem with cliques is two-fold. First, they are exclusionary, and second, they are populated by like-minded people, which can cause organizations to miss shifting environmental realities, particularly when the cliques wield social power. They are like office gangs that form to fill the gap left by inept leadership. Use the MBTI preferences described above as a lens through which you can observe cliques and become more welcoming of others. Be the model of behavior that undermines the influence of cliques in the organization.
- *Complacency within the team.* Provoke debates (not arguments) by encouraging others to offer differing views. Debates can bring forth a world of possibilities in an organization. When divergent views are presented in debates, people open up to viewpoints that challenge the status quo. Through debates a team of people can create a new common ground and a possibility for an emerging future.
- *Ideas within the team fall on deaf ears rather than being nurtured into something new or innovative.* When you don't welcome others' views it tends to sterilize innovation. Intentionally make fewer declarations, especially in meetings, and replace them with proposals – this way opening yourself up for challenge about what's possible. A declaration is a statement of your version of truth, e.g., "A weak marketing strategy is causing our sales to be flat." A proposal, on the other hand, is a statement of issue with some uncertainty about cause and effect. An example is, "Our sales are flat, and it may be due to a weak marketing strategy." Proposals encourage challenge between team members because the proposer is a catalyst for it. Instead of running ideas through technical filters, team members will respond to proposals by using their intuition and insights to connect the ideas of others into a picture of future possibilities.
- *The team does not meet often enough.* Group interactions are essential for rapport building, learning, knowledge sharing, providing/receiving guidance, and creating a sense of purpose and direction. Make meetings

among your team important by ensuring that certain decisions and actions require a group discussion. In this way the team meeting will become a core process. It can be the mode through which important guidance can be offered and shared across the team. To get started, you could institute a 30-minute "Monday morning" staff meeting. At the very least, and on an ongoing basis, each team member could provide a "check-in" on key projects and issues.

- *You do not ask for help.* Loosen up. Allow yourself to be vulnerable with people more often: ask for help, admit when you're worried, and apologize when you're wrong. Use vulnerability more tactically to enhance trust. You would do this with the same seven steps described above to deal with arrogance. (Read Brené Brown's book *Daring Greatly.*)

- *You are not likeable.* Seek insights about yourself from a few trusted associates. A collateral benefit of doing this will be improving your relationships. You will need to alter your conversational mode. Stop "telling" and engage others in an exchange of views whereby you are listening for how other people feel. By actively seeking the opinions of others you will be better able to understand and respond to how others think and feel.

- *Your team does not meet performance expectations.* Ask yourself, "Are you measuring the things that you expect people (yourself included) to deliver?" If the answer is no, go back to the goals set by the owners or board of directors and map them to what your team does. Create performance metrics for those things that map directly to the owner/board's goals. The team that you work with must be aligned around goals – ensure that it is. Be certain that every goal (what is to be achieved), has a metric (how it is to be achieved), which has a measure (how will it be measured), that has a target (what is the goal post).

- *You are reluctant to confront people when issues emerge.* Tolerance of poor performers and/or acceptance of unresolved disputes creates a lack of challenge in a team, enables mediocrity, and impairs motivation and morale. The improvement action is clear – stop postponing confrontations. It is a mindset change that requires practice. If a dispute emerges, use the Veritas Conversation described above. Practice the conversation with someone before actually confronting the poor performer. See what it feels like.

### 3. Create Key Processes

Most organizations recognize the importance of performance management yet do a lousy job of managing the process. A well-designed performance management system will maximize the potential of an organization and minimize interferences that get in the way of delivery. Reward systems must align behaviors within an organization while nurturing an environment of support that enhances motivation. Leaders ensure the behaviors that are desired are those rewarded. They understand the nuances that can derail a performance management system. They also understand that the selection of goals and metrics in performance management is absolutely critical because they ultimately shape the identity, purpose, and long-term viability of the organization. Leaders establish goals and metrics, as well as the strategies for developing the vital performance monitoring relationships between leaders and employees.

## Key Competencies

- Accountability
- Alignment
- Assurance
- Performance Management
- Rewards

## Common Issues and Suggested Improvement Actions

- *You are resistant to change.* Change should never be an objective in itself. The issue is that some challenges require adaptive solutions. Without an openness to change, you could miss the need to adapt to shifts in your environment. Increase the level of intuition in your decision-making. To do this you will need to balance intuition, data, and passions. Without intuition, you will either miss the need for adaptive changes, or be resistant to accept them. In addition, some of the greatest breakthroughs come from rigorous performance management. We suggest that you examine your mindset about performance management. Do you see it as more than assurance for current delivery? Do you see it as an enabler of change and continuous improvement? Look externally for motivation by becoming more aware of industry performance relative to each target set for the organization. Pursue becoming an industry leader rather than a mere participant.
- *You are not confident about your team's performance.* Engage your manager and team members in more frequent conversations about performance. At least have quarterly face-to-face conversations with your manager and then each direct report that you may have. In these conversations, test to make sure people have transparency about goals, metrics, measures, and targets. These conversations about performance will enhance individual accountability across the team and will create the opportunity for you to intervene in situations that need your support. There's a collateral benefit to having these performance-related conversations – everyone involved will feel more assured about their contributions to the delivery of the organization's goals and managers' expectations.
- *The context you share can be inappropriate and cause people to get the wrong messages.* Do an assessment of your personal message congruency. That is, make sure that the context that you share is consistent with the company's goals, performance management, and rewards systems. Don't situate your context; understand the context of your situation.

- *Too many interferences impair performance.* "Clear the decks." Make sure that people are not overwhelmed with too many objectives. Keep the performance formula clearly in mind, i.e., Performance = Potential − Interferences.[11] Examples of interferences include excessive demands that overwhelm minds; pessimism; unclear goals or conflicting messages; competition for limited resources; a volatile, uncertain, complex, or ambiguous (VUCA) environment. See if you can reduce the interferences. The rule of thumb that we express in our training programs is that people can do their day jobs and three things – more than three and we cannibalize effectiveness.

- *You're stuck in a narrow view of reality.* Understand that your organization's potential is shifting moment by moment as the internal and external environments shift through learning and adaptation. Put mechanisms around yourself (other people or processes) to constantly challenge what you believe, while maintaining the ability to react to the randomness of factors and influences. Always anticipate unawareness at the time of decision-making and the possibility of future information and factors.

- *You miss opportunities because too focused on a single goal.* Avoid being narrowly focused on one goal. The risk is that a single goal could create "goalodicy" i.e., when a goal shapes your or the organization's collective identity.[12] In such cases, opportunities can be missed, or emerging issues can be overlooked. Create a balanced score card with multiple and dovetailed goals.

- *People are in distress with unattainable goals.* In order for performance management to be most effective there must be clear goals, i.e., what you want people to achieve. Make sure that the goals are actually attainable – aspiration is a great thing but we don't want to put people in a state of distress by having too many goals or ones that are impossible to achieve. The idea is to get people into a "zone" where they have just enough challenge but not so much that they are overwhelmed.

- *Performance of your team or organization has fallen behind peers in the industry.* Look externally for inspiration by becoming more aware of your competitors' performance relative to each target you are setting for your organization. Looking internally tends to drive incremental improvement while external perspectives can create step-change and/or breakthrough outcomes.

- *Your team shies away from accountability.* People must take accountability for the outcomes they create. In order to do so, they must have authority sufficient for the decisions and actions that they must take to deliver on their responsibilities. If there is a gap between delegated authority and responsibility, then there is no accountability.

- *You're seen as unwilling to delegate authority to others.* There's often a fear aspect in delegating authority. Sometimes technical experts, or people new to management roles, fear losing grip or control over a critical process or operation. They fear that people to whom they delegate lack either the required skills or the willingness to be accountable. This can be overcome by implementing a rigorous performance management and monitoring system. The other fear, in its worst form, is called "inferiority psychosis." This occurs when a person feels that their skill set is not up to the mark and will be surpassed by someone to whom they delegate authority. Everyone encounters thoughts and feelings of inadequacy from time to time and seeking feedback from trusted colleagues can help. In a chronic situation, we suggest getting help from a therapist.

- *You have a poor understanding of how pay systems affect performance.* Pay systems help to align employees with an organization's goals. These systems are not necessarily motivational. Make sure that you understand the criticality of teamwork and functional excellence in pay system design. Remember: you get what you reward. If you are hoping for collaboration and teamwork yet rewarding individuals for their achievements over others, then you will not get teamwork or collaboration.
- *You could be more open about mistakes and learning.* Only people who do things make mistakes. Look for what can be learned from mistakes that you and others make. Share these learnings generously and broadly with others, this way allowing yourself to be more vulnerable. Doing this will enhance your trust and credibility in the organization.

## 4. Steward Structure

We typically think of organization structure as a description of who does what and who reports to whom. Organization structure is much more than a formal system of internal tasks and reporting relationships – something that shows up on organization charts or on websites. Leaders understand that structure must be carefully matched to the organization's purpose and environment. Structure also creates the links among authority, responsibility, and accountability. Structure influences behavior and shapes an organization's culture over time, much like a skeleton gives shape to a body and allows movement. Leaders use structure judiciously as an enabler of change; they know how it can be aligned appropriately to nurture effective behavior and reporting relationships. Caution must be exercised in order to avoid misguided structure change.

### Key Competencies

- Tweaks
- Restructurings
- Mechanistic Structure
- Organic Structure
- Matrix Structure

### Common Issues and Suggested Improvement Actions

- *You put too much emphasis on structure as a problem or a solution.* Leaders often change or talk about changing the organization structure too often and to too large an extent. Seeing issues at work through a lens of hierarchy and structure can create a biased perspective, as if it is a "cure all" for every problem. Most work issues are about poor conversations, poor relationships, ineffective performance management, and inadequate networks. We have two reading suggestions. First, read Element 4 in *Becoming a Leader*. Next, read Niall Ferguson's *The Square and the Tower*. These two readings could shape a new outlook for you.

- *You might be missing opportunities to refine structure.* Be more tactical with small changes in organization structure, either those that you make or suggest to others. There are always opportunities to tweak structure to improve efficiency or effectiveness. Great leaders use subtle changes in organization structure to improve performance.

- *You are reluctant to deal with people who don't fit what's needed for the team.* Act more decisively with people who do not have the skill sets needed to meet the functional requirements of your organization. In this situation, the structure is right, but the people are not the right fit which enables mediocrity, impairs morale and ultimately the viability of the team. Some issues can be handled on your own; others require your boss's help – either way it is an honest conversation on your part.

- *Authority delegation is either insufficient or blurred.* As noted above, if people do not have authority commensurate with their responsibility, they won't take accountability. Review position descriptions (starting with yours) to ensure that each person has sufficient authority to make decisions relative to their responsibilities.

### 5. Set Boundaries

Boundaries define right and wrong – without them individuals lose their way and organizational anxiety ensues. This can create confusion, conflicts, paralysis, and cannibalization of energy. Leaders create Code-of-Conduct policies and manage these proactively rather than in damage control when a crisis occurs. Employee welfare is paramount for leaders, and the boundaries they set and enforce ensure this. Leaders are mindful of the messages sent to others in the organization through their own behavior. It is a leader's job to get all employees into positions where they can continuously learn and this requires inclusion – the state where each employee feels valued, respected, and supported. Continuous learning (referred to as learning loops) is used to ensure inclusion and to promote employee welfare. To the extent possible every aspect of an employee's job should be an opportunity to learn. In this way every employee achieves his or her highest potential, and not just a chosen few.

### Key Competencies

- License to Operate
- Employee Welfare
- Inclusion

*Common Issues and Suggested Improvement Actions*

- *Guidelines about good and bad behavior are unclear*. Review your organization's Code of Conduct. Does it accurately reflect the values you want to demonstrate? Is it being rigorously enforced? Does anyone know what is in it? Look for opportunities to talk about it with other employees. Be clear about your expectations of good and bad behavior, particularly as it relates to aspects of the Code of Conduct. Make sure you are acknowledging people based on merit and not ignoring bad behavior by good performers.
- *Work is not perceived as a learning opportunity*. Do more to encourage learning by presenting jobs as opportunities for continuous improvement. You can affect a person's attitude about their potential by giving them opportunities to learn. If you are accountable for employees, make sure that every person on your team has opportunities to learn – no dead-end jobs. Each person should be in a learning loop customized for their needs.
- *You are not seen as modelling safe work practices and behaviors*. Be aware that your behavior does not have a neutral gear – it is always affecting someone. Regardless of how you feel about your organization's safety programs and initiatives, or the level of your direct involvement in either, you must always be seen as aware and supportive. There can be no gaps between what the organization espouses about safety and the way you behave. There have been tons of studies done about safety management over the years and one thing is clear – most managers are not good at safety conversations. Bottom line: if you're not talking about safety in the workplace then you are not leading in the matter of safety.
- *Harassment is tolerated in the workplace*. Take the initiative to ensure that the organization's Code of Conduct addresses *Harassment* and explicitly *Toxic Behaviors*. The #MeToo movement has created heightened awareness on one hand, which is a good thing, and confusion on the other about what is "toxic." At the same time, the community at large has become increasing intolerant of anything that is perceived as "toxic." It only takes one mistake to destroy a management's reputation with employees, customers, and the board.
- *You are seen as treating employees unfairly*. Ensure fairness in recognizing the accomplishments of others, and how development opportunities are allocated to employees. Be acutely aware that you will tend to focus recognition on those who are a reflection of yourself – it is a weakness that must be managed. To the extent that you have influence, make sure that compensation is tied to demonstrated competency and achievement.

## Four Elements of Personal Leadership Competency

### 1. Nurture Behaviors

Nothing a leader says or does is ignored. Leaders are always on stage whether they want to be or not. A leader's behavior speaks more loudly than his or her voice. It is never neutral. It is contagious, can ignite passion, evoke trust, and inspire success. It can also promote incivility, unethical, or toxic behavior if misguided and mismanaged (see Box 1.3 Ethical Leadership). Leaders must manage their behavior – it is not a consequence of who they are – it is an input to what they can be. It demonstrates what they believe and value. Three components of leadership behavior – integrity, courage, and intolerance – are critical. The role of emotional intelligence is equally important. Emotional intelligence is defined as "the capability of a person to manage and control his or her emotions and possess the ability to control the emotions of others as well. In other words, they can influence the emotions of other people also."[13] It includes five components: self-awareness, self-regulation, motivation, empathy, and sociability.[14] As individuals progress in their careers the technical skills that made them stand out initially become less significant and are replaced by a need for critical leadership behaviors. Developing these behavioral patterns is less about innate ability and more about being true to yourself and having a growth mindset. The model for deliberative behavior change is: Change = (Experience + Expectation) * Attention * Veto Power.[15] Literally, to change your behavior, you must practice the behavior that you want in order for it to become automatic (Experience); believe that you can do it (Expectation); practice the new behavior in all aspects of your life (Attention); and stop all of the behaviors that are holding you back (Veto Power).

*Key Competencies*

- Courage
- Integrity
- Intolerance
- Self-Awareness
- Self-Regulation
- Motivation
- Empathy
- Sociability

## Box 1.3: Ethical Leadership

Ethical behavior in an organization is paramount to its reputation, its ability to attract customers and ultimately to its success.[16] However, according to the Ethics Resource Center's 2012 national business ethics survey of Fortune 500 employees, over half of workers reported having observed misconduct.[17] Leadership at all levels is critical to the ethical behavior of employees and to the ethical climate in the organization. Ethical leadership is defined as "the demonstration of normatively appropriate conduct through personal actions and interpersonal relationships and the promotion of such conduct to followers through two-way communication, reinforcement and decision-making."[18]

Leaders need to demonstrate the highest moral standards in their communications, actions, decisions, and behaviors both within and outside the workplace (moral manager, and moral person). Ethical leaders signal to employees the types of behaviors that are expected and valued, and those that will be rewarded and punished. Ignoring bad behavior essentially sanctions it.

A great deal of prior research has drawn attention to the importance of leadership and role models in shaping the behavior of employees.[18,19] Two classic leaders considered as good examples of ethical leadership are James Burke who led Johnson & Johnson during the Tylenol crisis and Bill George retired CEO of Medtronic. Bill George is the author of *Discover Your True North* and currently is on the faculty at Harvard.[20] One way that leaders impact the ethical behavior of their followers is by creating an ethical climate. Ethical climate refers to employees' perceptions that the organization's values and beliefs about morality are shared by employees in that organization. Essentially, ethical leadership creates the ethical climate which influences how individuals behave.[21] Through role modeling, rewards, punishments, and communication leaders maintain (or fail to maintain) a moral ethical climate. For example, Mayer and colleagues found that employee misconduct was greater when the ethical climate was weak.[22] The Ethics Resource Center (ERC) in 2005 found that when top managers demonstrated ethical behavior, employees were 50 percent less likely to act unethically.[23] An example of this in the survey was "Top management in my company has let it be known in no uncertain terms that unethical behaviors will not be tolerated."[24]

Trust in the leader is also a critical component influencing the extent to which individuals are motivated to perform and to behave ethically. Untrustworthy leaders are not respected. Trust exists when the leader is reliable and can be counted on to do what they say they will do; open, sharing as much information as possible; competent; and compassionate – working to meet the needs of others.[25]

Also of interest, Elango and colleagues found that younger employees were more likely to be influenced by organizational ethical climate and they were also less likely than older managers to make ethical choices.[24] This suggests that younger employees are highly susceptible to the leadership they experience and this needs to be considered.

Bottom line: inspire trust in others and role model ethical behavior, thereby creating an ethical climate, and use communication, rewards, and punishments accordingly and employees will be far more likely to behave ethically.

## Common Issues and Suggested Improvement Actions

- *You do not manage your behavior wisely.* Always keep in mind that your behavior is not neutral; it is either taking people up or it is taking them down. Your behavior is not a consequence of who you are – it is input to what you can be. Actively manage your behavior as if it is the most important ingredient in your success.
- *You lack courage in decision-making.* Find courage through the practice of a "Stoic Pause." A Stoic Pause, in this context, is a moment when you visualize the outcomes from not making a decision. In this way you suspend emotional judgment and focus objectively on the consequences of non-action or delaying a decision, i.e., regrets. You find courage by considering how bad things will get if you don't act or don't decide.
- *You could nurture more engagement among team members.* Start monitoring other people's body language when they are around you and learn to

perceive how people are reacting to you emotionally. Do people seem genuinely happy to see you? Do they want to engage you in conversations? Are they making eye contact, or do they seem to want to avoid you? This monitoring alone will broaden your awareness and help you to refine your interactions with others.

- *You are not proactive in shaping an environment where people feel optimistic.* Words matter. Expressing gratefulness for what you have or what's been accomplished is important. Talking about possibilities imparts a level of optimism. In meetings, take note if you play the role of "devil's advocate" too much. The next time a colleague proposes an initiative, take the time to consider their perspective and their contribution. Temper your initial reaction with positive statements, like "that sounds promising," or "did you consider the alternative."

- *You are not seen as a good role model for leadership behaviors.* Either complete an Emotional Intelligence assessment (e.g., www.ihhp.com/free-eq-quiz/) or review the one you have. Create a two-month plan to practice new behaviors for the areas of weakness, while deploying more effort on the strengths. Practice improvements on weaknesses by starting in smaller "safe" groups and building out to larger settings. Practice at home, at work, in the community, and in all of your personal environments.

- *You could be more inquisitive.* Ask more questions – this way you create an opportunity to discover new insights that might spark fresh ideas. Suspend judgment when you are listening to people, and you will ultimately allow yourself to be receptive to what someone is saying. Lastly, step out of the past more often. When you focus too much on the past, you don't give yourself a chance to be curious about the future.

- *You are not seen as happy.* Step back from the robotic aspects of your life and identify your key motivators – often these reflect your deepest beliefs. (Complete the SCARF assessment noted earlier.) Identify the aspects of your current situation that "scratch the itch" of what motivates you. Consider the options you have for those aspects that are not enjoyable. Take control of your situation.

- *You are missing the triggers that cause you to challenge your beliefs.* Sharpen your critical thinking skills through learning more about what's at issue, reading more, and listening better. Challenge what you believe by always searching for the most informed viewpoint. Do this by making more proposals to people that invite challenge. Be aware that you have created your reality and you can be blinded by it. We all tend to seek and believe information that confirms what we believe to be true.

- *You could be calmer from time to time.* Try harder to control or redirect impulses and moods: breathe, think, and then act. You may not be aware of your stressors. Share more about your feelings and concerns with people, generally being more vulnerable. It takes practice. Start with people you know well – see what it feels like to be vulnerable. Tactically, you would do this with the following steps: (1) from time to time admit that you're not the best at everything – or anything, (2) acknowledge your own faults, (3) express gratefulness for what you have, and (4) don't be afraid to acknowledge when situations concern you. Before you say something … anything … pass it through three gates: Is it true? Is it kind? Is it useful?[26]

- *Unaware of the feelings of others*. During every conversation see if you can anticipate what a person wants to say before they say it. A good way into this is to listen to others for things that you don't know rather than confirmation of what you already believe. Suspend judgment of people, especially when things go wrong, and try to understand why a problem exists. See if you can identify the emotional needs of the people involved before you act. Monitor other people's body language more closely when they are around you and learn to understand how people are reacting to you emotionally. The act of listening like this conveys a sense of warmth and caring.
- *Unaware of implicit gender biases*. Become more aware of the masculine and feminine energy reflected in your personal and organizational biases by completing a Versatility Factor assessment at www.versatili-tyfactor.com/freeassessment. Download the *Improvement Guide* from the website. Evaluate your V-Factor Profile and use the guide's template to identify a daily practice for improvement.

## 2. Conversations

Everything that occurs in an organization happens as a result of conversations. These conversations are often spent dwelling on the past or focusing on our immediate situation. A leader's life must extend the focus of conversations into the future. Clearly, lessons from the past cannot be ignored, but they must only be used as fuel for what is important, namely the future. Leaders are accessible through conversations. Conversations within an organization turn it into a viable and living network of people, with the highest level of teamwork enabled by future-oriented conversations. Becoming aware of self-narratives – those conversations going on in our own heads – is a powerful way for leaders to emerge from the past and to see new possibilities for others and the organization. Leaders launch conversations into possibilities through their language, and by being self-observers of labels and truths. They consciously control their listening by suspending judgments and not being blinded by their image of themselves.

### Key Competencies

- Future Domain
- Proposal
- Veritas
- Performance Monitoring
- Debate

- Dialogue
- Context Setting
- Coaching

## Common Issues and Suggested Improvement Actions

- *Your speaking style shuts down creativity.* Words matter. Speaking in absolutes with words like, "will," "cannot," and "must" limits potential. Leaders evoke future possibilities in conversations by inviting them with words like, "what if," "how could," "could it be" …
- *You talk too much and listen too little.* From time to time intentionally stop talking in meetings, sit quietly, and just listen to others speak. Let the dialogue mature among the members before you jump into the conversation. When you do jump in, ask others what they think rather than sharing your views. Practice the "Big Four": (1) be aware of and value what listeners bring to the conversation, (2) pay attention to what it feels like to be listened to and not get lost in your own head, (3) feel gratitude for listeners who acknowledge you, and (4) be aware of the well-being of the listeners.
- *You can be stubborn from time to time.* Read Annie Duke's book, *Thinking in Bets*. She articulates an argument for adopting some variation of "I'm not sure" versus "I know the answers and I'm right."[27] Her point is that acknowledging uncertainty is the first step in achieving a goal of getting closer to what is objective truth. Learn to be comfortable with the world being uncertain and unpredictable. Don't focus on being sure, rather figure out how unsure you are. When you move away from the world of right and wrong, you start living in the continuum between the extremes, and decision-making becomes about how well you calibrate among all the shades of grey.
- *You say things that are inappropriate or leave people in a bad place.* Saying things that don't land well is all about self-narratives. It is easy to be in a meeting or when someone is talking, to let your mind wander into crafting the perfect response, and you talk to yourself about what you believe or "your story." Once the person finishes their thought, you reengage and share your perfect rebuttal – but it is totally out of pace with where the conversation has gone or what the person had just said to you. Practice getting out of your head in conversations, listen better, and allow yourself to be totally present – master the art of presence.
- *You are seen as disrespectful.* Be more affirming when talking to people by using the following four steps: (1) give them eye contact and encourage non-verbal's like nodding, (2) acknowledge the opinions of others even though you might not agree with them, (3) don't monopolize speaking time, e.g., limit yourself to no more than three minutes per topic, and (4) don't say something that you know is untrue, unkind, or not useful.
- *You are perceived as moody from time to time.* The issue with being seen as moody is that people will be wary of you. Why? They don't know which

version of you is going to show up. One way into this is to show more commitment to what you do. Be more determined, sincerely devoted to your work, and enthusiastic about your team's contribution to the company. This way you will have to be more aware of your moods when you enter the workplace, and more diligent in managing them.

- *You do not ask enough questions in conversations.* Provoke new insights for yourself by asking more questions. We coach people to use the three-successive-question style: ask the first question, then another as a follow-up, and then a third that digs even deeper. This way you create an opportunity to discover new insights that might spark fresh ideas. Don't do this as a "cross examination" where you already know what you're going after. Rather, suspend judgment when you are listening to people, and you will ultimately allow yourself to be receptive to what someone is saying. When you focus too much on your own perspectives, you don't give yourself a chance to be curious about what other people are saying.

### 3. Provide Support

Anyone who has been in the workforce for some time can likely remember a situation when they did not feel they had their boss's support. It may not have been an obvious lack of support, but the "feeling" just wasn't there. Support is a process that starts with a conversation. These conversations can be the beginning of a genuine relationship that ultimately will develop into a mutually supportive process. Leaders realize that their mental and emotional proximity to another person will impact that person's perceptions of support and, as a result, their development potential. Opportunities emerge for employees when leaders nurture relationships with them. Leaders and their support are the agents of employee learning and development, which are the building blocks of organizational success. The leader's belief in an employee's success is also a powerful motivator (see Box 1.4 Pygmalion: Self-fulfilling Prophecy of High Expectations).

### Key Competencies

- People Relationships
- Storytelling
- Friendships
- Credibility

## Box 1.4:  Pygmalion: Self-fulfilling Prophecy of High Expectations

Do our expectations for others' behavior or performance influence what they accomplish? A classic experiment conducted by Rosenthal and Jacobson demonstrated that, indeed, expectations of another do impact what that person does.[28] These psychologists gave elementary school children an IQ test. They then told the children's teachers that certain students had great aptitude and would show remarkable progress in the coming year. They labeled these students "intellectual bloomers." In reality these students were selected entirely at random. Another group was labeled average. When the students were given a second test at the end of the year, those labeled bloomers did significantly better than the students labeled average. The explanation given was that the teachers' expectations had affected their own behavior toward the "bloomers," which in turn encouraged the students to perform to the expectations. This phenomenon is labeled the self-fulfilling prophecy or Pygmalion effect. King first demonstrated a similar effect in a non-school setting.[29] Eden and Shani demonstrated a similar effect with soldiers and their leaders. Soldiers who were expected to perform better did so, even though their capabilities did not differ.[30] The influence of expectations has even been extended to seasickness ... those who were told they had a psychological profile that suggested they would not get seasick performed better and reported less seasickness than those not told such.[31]

## Golem – Self-fulfilling Prophecy of Low Expectations

The Golem effect is the term coined by Babad, Inbar, and Rosenthal for the negative version of Pygmalion. The Golem effect is Pygmalion in reverse.[32] Managers' low expectations for followers can decrease follower performance. Reynolds designed a study in which teachers in a management class were led to believe they were assigned either lower-performing or higher-performing students based on a pre-test.[33] Actually, the students were randomly chosen to be labeled lower or higher performing. He showed that students labeled lower performing actually performed worse on a post-test and the students labeled higher performing did better.

---

### *Common Issues and Suggested Improvement Actions*

- *You do not initiate conversations with people about their development.* Have more coaching conversations, even with peers and your boss. Make it real and not a "tick in the box" effort. In order to coach people, you need to: meet them on their turf, with good eye contact, giving them freedom to choose, engaging them with questions, understanding their motivations, and acknowledging their effort. Being on their turf is not only about their physical space but also about trying to get into their emotional mindset. Your perspective should be that you can co-create a person's future by having conversations with them about their potential. Don't force fit people into a model of what you think is appropriate; help them find access to their full potential. Also, don't direct their careers but rather encourage them to take control of their future with whatever support you can provide. A self-directed future is way more powerful than one that's dictated.
- *You could do more to help people find new possibilities for themselves.* Read about the Relationship Support Matrix in Element 7 (Support) in *Becoming a Leader*. Pick five people in your work environment and plot your relationship with them on the Relationship Support Matrix. For those relationships that are not in the Healthy quadrant, intentionally shift

your listening to be more empathic and/or shift the field pattern into more dialogues. Initially, ask questions in a way that helps the person explain how they feel about a given situation. If they don't respond accordingly, explain your feelings as a way to evoke the same from them.

- *You discourage others from being authentic.* Be aware that you will judge people based on your biases, and force-fit them into a model of what you think is appropriate. Suspend your current truth about people, especially during coaching conversations. Let the conversation become a convergence of possibilities from which potential actions are co-created for the person to exercise choice. Try to be more empathetic and realize that you may not know what is going on with another person. All you see is their behavior. Log into http://courses.washington.edu/pbaf-hall/514/514%20Readings/2008%20Self%20and%20Other%20Pronin.pdf and read "How we see ourselves and how we see others."

- *You are weak at storytelling.* Start giving people a hint of the emotional tenor of your speaking. You can say: "Hey, I've got some good news to share," or "I'm in a bind here and could use some advice." Create a handful of short stories that convey key learnings from your life. Use these stories to convey messages that are not force-fed but help the listener reach their own conclusion.

- *Your voice does not inspire credibility.* Get feedback about your voice volume from someone who knows you well. Also, download the Vocular App so you can practice different voice frequencies and immediately see their effect. Manage your voice volume to ensure that it is neither too high nor too low. Explore pitch management techniques and options if your frequency exceeds 125 Hz.

- *Overly focused on friendships at work.* You must have relationships at work but be careful with friendships as these can create opportunities for abuse and manipulation. Read *No Hard Feelings* by Liz Fosslien and Mollie West Duffy. The authors discuss three types of work friendships: (1) *confidants* with whom we commiserate, (2) *inspirations* who we use as mentors, and (3) *frenemies* who are like us and we use as benchmarks for what we could be.[34] Of the three, an over-reliance on *confidants* tends to create problems at work when trust is either misplaced or breached.

## *4. Space to Deliver*

The final step in a leader's journey is often the most elusive – give employees space by stepping back and letting them deliver. The objective is to step back, but not step away. Leaders shift their focus from the work of delivery onto the work of people. What leaders do to achieve their own mastery, they must also use to nurture the people around them. Their ongoing effort is focused on staying in the future, interrogating reality, managing behavior, having conversations, monitoring performance, and providing support to people and the organization.

*Key Competency*

- Step Back but Not Away

*Common Issues and Suggested Improvement Actions*

- *You are seen as overly controlling.* Remember that a leader's job is to focus on the people who do the work rather than the work itself. You do this through six ongoing actions: (1) sustain conversations about the future and possibilities, (2) make proposals and not directives, (3) model the behaviors that you want others to adopt, (4) share context liberally throughout the organization, (5) monitor performance rigorously, and (6) create support with people by having conversations with them about their potential.
- *You do not describe a viable future.* Never forget that your relationship with the organization is driven by the messages inferred from what you say and do about the future. Congruent messages about direction, performance, and boundaries must exist from the top to the bottom of the organization. Your messages will not be believed if your credibility is impaired, thus you must always be diligent about managing your integrity, never stepping over the fine line. You may not have all of the information for all situations, but you can share your context generously to help others deal with the situations they encounter. To evoke passion, you must be succinct in describing the direction for the future. In less than 60 seconds be prepared to say about the organization: where are we going, who's going with us, why are we going there, what are we doing to get there, and when will we arrive.

## FINAL WORDS

We are going to draw a line at this point on coaching comments about leadership issues and improvement actions. A total of 65 have been highlighted. Our hope is that readers of *Becoming a Leader* will have been reminded of the Nine Elements of Leadership Mastery (and acknowledge the new acronym NELM) and new readers will have enough of an introduction to the 43 NELM competencies to move forward with the rest of this book. We also hope that all readers will reflect on the coaching comments and find access to resolve challenges in their leadership journey.

## References

1   Groff, Jonathan (2015). *Hamilton: An American Musical*. Atlantic Records.
2   Kruger, J., & Dunning, D. (1999). "Unskilled and unaware of it: How difficulties in recognizing one's own incompetence lead to inflated self-assessments." *Journal of Personality and Social Psychology*, 77(6), 1121–1134.
3   Scott, S. (2004). *Fierce conversations: Achieving success at work and in life, one conversation at a time*. New York, NY: Berkley Publishing Group.

4   Clark, T. (2020). *The 4 stages of psychological safety.* Oakland, CA: Barett-Koehler.

5   Muraven, M., & Slessareva, E. (2003). Mechanisms of self-control failure: Motivation and limited resources. *Personality and Social Psychology Bulletin, 29*(7), 894–906.

6   *Psychology Today* (n.d.). Retrieved April 6, 2020 from www.psychologytoday. com/us/blog/changepower/201603/know-yourself-6-specific-ways-know-who-you-are.

7   McCarthy, A., & Garavan, T. (1999). Developing self-awareness in the managerial career development process: The value of 360-degree feedback and the MBTI. *Journal of European Industrial Training, 23*(9), 437–445.

8   Kirwan Institute for the Study of Race and Ethnicity (n.d.). Retrieved April 6, 2020 from http://kirwaninstitute.osu.edu/research/understanding-implicit-bias/.

9   Verywell Mind (n.d.) Retrieved April 6, 2020 from www.verywellmind.com/ implicit-bias-overview-4178401.

10   Malinen, S., & Johnston, L. (2013). Workplace ageism: Discovering hidden bias. *Experimental Aging Research, 39*(4), 445–465.

11   Gallwey, W. T. (2001). *The inner game of work: Focus, learning, pleasure, and mobility in the workplace.* New York, NY: Random House Publishing Group.

12   Kayes, D. C. (2006). *Destructive goal pursuit: The Mt. Everest disaster.* New York, NY: Palgrave Macmillan.

13   *The Economic Times* (2020). Retrieved April 1, 2020 from https://economictimes. indiatimes.com/definition/emotional-intelligence

14   Goleman, D. P. (1998). What makes a leader? *Harvard Business Review, 76*(6), 93–102.

15   Rock, D., & Page, L. J. (2009). *Coaching with the brain in mind: Foundations for practice.* Hoboken, NJ: Wiley.

16   Lu, C., & Lin, C. (2014). The effects of ethical leadership and ethical climate on employee ethical behavior in the international port context. *Journal of Business Ethics, 124,* 209–223.

17   Ethics Resource Center (2012). *National Business Ethics Survey of Fortune 500 Employees.* Washington, DC: Ethics Resource Center.

18   Brown, M., Trevino, L., & Harrison, D. (2005). Ethical leadership: A social learning perspective for construct development and testing. *Organizational Behavior and Human Decision Processes, 97*(2), 117–134.

19   Toor, S., & Ofori, G. (2009). Ethical leadership: Examining the relationships with full range leadership model, employee outcomes and organizational culture. *Journal of Business Ethics, 90*(4), 533–547.

20   Bello, S. (2012). Impact of ethical leadership on employee job performance. *International Journal of Business and Social Science, 3,* 228–236.

21   Trevino, L., Butterfield, K., & McCabe, D. (1998). The ethical context in organizations: Influences on employee attitudes and behaviors. *Business Ethics Quarterly, 8*(3), 447–476.

22   Mayer, D., Kuenzi, M., Greenbaum, R., Bardes, M., & Salvador, R. (2009). How low does ethical leadership flow? Test of a trickle-down model. *Organizational Behavior and Human Decision Processes, 108*(1), 1–13.

23   Ethics Resource Center (2005). National *Business Ethics Survey: How Employees View Ethics in Their Organizations.* Washington, DC: Ethics Resource Center.

24   Elango, B., Paul, K., Kundu, S., & Paudel, S. (2010). Organizational ethics, individual ethics, and ethical intentions in international decision-making. *Journal of Business Ethics, 97,* 543–561, p. 558.

25    Mishra, A., & Mishra, K. (2012). *Becoming a trustworthy leader: Psychology and practice.* New York, NY: Brunner-Routledge.

26    davidji. (2015). *destressifying.* Notting Hill Gate, London: Hay House UK Ltd.

27    Duke, A. (2018). *Thinking in bets.* New York, NY: Penguin.

28    Rosenthal, R., & Jacobson, L. (1968). *Pygmalion in the classroom: Teacher expectation and pupils' intellectual development.* New York, NY: Holt, Rinehart & Winston.

29    King, A. S. (1971). Self-fulfilling prophecies in training the hard-core: Supervisors' expectations and the underprivileged workers' performance. *Social Science Quarterly, 52*(2), 369–378.

30    Eden, D., & Shani, A. B. (1982). Pygmalion goes to boot camp: Expectancy, leadership, and trainee performance. *Journal of Applied Psychology, 67*(2), 194–199.

31    Eden, D., & Yaakov Zuk, D. (1995). Seasickness as a self-fulfilling prophecy: Raising self-efficacy to boost performance at sea. *Journal of Applied Psychology, 80*(5), 628–635.

32    Babad, E. Y., Inbar, J., & Rosenthal, R. (1982). Pygmalion, Galatea, and the Golem: Investigations of biased and unbiased teachers. *Journal of Educational Psychology, 74*(4), 459–474.

33    Reynolds, D. (2007). "Restraining Golem and harnessing Pygmalion in the classroom: A laboratory study of managerial expectations and task design." *Academy of Management Learning & Education, 6*(4), 475–483.

34    Fosslien, L., & West Duffy, M. (2019). *No Hard Feelings.* New York, NY: Penguin.

# 2  THE **HOLY** GRAIL

The title of the previous chapter is *Back to the Future* and we have done just that, i.e., we have gone to the past – *Becoming a Leader* – and now want to return to the present – *Deepening the Journey*. But there is one more aspect of the past that we need to address, and that's feedback about NELM from readers and clients over the years. We have received a range of views. Some think it is the "holy grail" of leadership and transforms culture when implemented successfully in organizations. Others feel that it reflects an aspiration to pursue godliness for mankind, while still others believe that it is a cloaked form of Machiavellianism. Let us explore these views.

## NELM: GODLINESS OR MACHIAVELLIAN?

We are often challenged in our training programs by participants who feel that the act of managing one's behavior is disingenuous and manipulative, and a far cry from the authenticity advocated by us as good leadership behavior. The Machiavellian label has been cast about. In *Becoming a Leader*, we explain that authenticity is about who we are in the moment and managing behavior is about practicing the behaviors that will shape who we can be. As noted by *Dilbert* comic strip creator, Scott Adams, "Never be yourself if you can make yourself into something better through your conscious actions."[1] However, we understand how readers could infer that some of the practices advocated by Machiavelli are similar to those we suggest, and we would like to clear up the confusion.

In other instances, impassioned attendees argue that NELM is just another way of describing godliness. The view is that if one strips away from their thought process all spiritual and human images of god, and views god as a concept, what emerges is NELM. Stated alternatively, the concepts of leadership espoused in *Becoming a Leader* are the same concepts one sees in god (i.e., perfection).

We will explore both here and try to elucidate how our espoused model of leadership may reflect, to some extent, Machiavellianism and godliness.

### Is Machiavellianism Consistent with NELM?

First, let us review and dissect Machiavelli's writings about power (or leadership) by examining *The Prince*, the text written by Niccolò Machiavelli in 1513.[2]

DOI: 10.4324/9781003036791-2

Laced with 26 chapters of reasoned thinking, Machiavelli weaves together perspectives about the nature of people and leaders who rule over them consistent with the politics and beliefs of the time.

Let us first point out that there are many interpretations of Machiavelli's writings in *The Prince*. The book was actually published in 1532, 19 years after its writing and five years after his death. Some believe that he was advocating brutal and outlandish treatment of followers as the way to power. Others have speculated that it was written so the depraved leader at the time (who actually followed his advice) would be so hated that it would bring about his own ruin. It is speculated that he was hoping his rival leaders, the Medici family, would adhere to his advice and fail. Others believe that Machiavelli was a satirist telling people about the mechanics of power they should fear and resist. Still others hold that it is a work about philosophy in which truth is more important than ideals, and there are clear leadership principles that are worthy of heeding, though they must be considered in light of the time in which he wrote. Below we will review the mindset and behaviors Machiavelli believed rulers had to adopt in order to govern.

### *Nature of People*

In expounding on the nature of people Machiavelli addresses behavior, reality, greed, self-interest, values, motivation, and commitment. Here is a summary of his perspectives:

- *About Behavior.* People are self-centered and self-interested. They will imitate the behavior of those they admire. In the end, individuals will judge results, and if these are favorable to them, it makes little matter how they were achieved. In this way, ends justify means. Regardless of the means, people will be praised when they succeed in attempts to acquire or achieve; when mishaps occur, they will be blamed. Moreover, people will accept the worst of behaviors from those in positions of power, provided that these behaviors are short lived and seen as benefitting either them or the community's best interest. They will even align with an oppressor if such a person ultimately treats them well. Because people are quick to change their nature when they believe they can improve their lot, leaders must also be shrewd. People know the difference between good behavior (generous, courteous, loyal, sincere, tenderhearted, humane, and honorable) and bad behavior (greedy, cruel, arrogant, deceitful, frivolous, and distrustful), but they are willing to align with the bad if it serves their self-interest. He also states that cruelty can be better than kindness, "making an example of one or two offenders is kinder than being too compassionate and allowing disorders to develop into murder and chaos which affects the whole community."[3]
- *About Reality.* Reality is elusive and much of it is based on imagination rather than what has actually been seen or known to exist. It is largely a construction of the mind and tied to what a person chooses to observe. In

Machiavelli's words, "Men in general judge rather by the eye than by the hand, for everyone can see but few can touch."[2] As a result, people will tend to miss the opportunity to influence the reality that they experience. Instead, they will rely too heavily on fate and less on their own efforts for success in life. As quoted, "I think it may be the case that Fortune (luck) is the mistress of one half our actions, and yet leaves the control of the other half, or a little less, to ourselves."[2]

- *About Greed and Self-Interest.* People are driven by their present needs and will act in any way, good or bad, to achieve them. They are thankless, fickle, risk adverse, and greedy to gain. They will be a devoted supporter as long as it benefits them and will readily turn against a benefactor when they think it is in their best interest. As a result, friendships are shallow, and betrayal is likely at any time.

- *About Values, Motivation, and Commitment.* People value self-determination along with wealth and power. As quoted, "a person will sooner forget the death of a loved one than the loss of their wealth and property."[2] When people are accustomed to having freedom and the ability to exercise choice, they will fight to retain it. Those who have nothing will fight the hardest to advance themselves because they have little to lose and everything to gain. Whereas, those who are well off will value the status quo; and they can become complacent and seek no further growth.

  Commitment has a lot to do with a person's state of mind – idle minds tend to build conspiracies; busy minds are preoccupied with what is at hand. People will feel committed not only from the benefits that they receive from a community but also from the effort they put into it. In this way, money alone does not secure the loyalty and commitment of people; they must feel part of the community from which they benefit.

Are Machiavelli's proclamations about human nature relatable to those embedded in NELM, 500 years later? Yes, for the most part. He concludes that people know the difference between good and bad behavior and are prepared to align with whatever advances their self-interest. Sadly, we have too many examples in all walks of life where this has been played out. Thus, it is naïve to believe all will behave ethically, morally, and humanely. At times cruelty (punishment) is the only option to enforce boundaries and remove toxicity from the workplace. Some of his ideas are also consistent with the notion of the importance of performance management, reward systems, and leading by example as we advocate.

His ideas about reality often being based on imagination and what people want to believe also aligns with our notion of the need to interrogate reality. Machiavelli believed that goals and objectives needed to be morally based (virtuous) but he did not believe all activities to achieve them also needed to be virtuous. We differ in that we think that values should guide goals, *and* they also need to be the basis for the behaviors that get them accomplished.

## *Leaders*

Now let us explore Machiavelli's assertion about leaders, which he describes as princes, or people who have power and influence over others. "Machiavellian" is a label associated with unscrupulous behaviors such as manipulation, emotional coldness, indifference to morality; characterized by subtle cunning, deception, expediency, and dishonesty. It is often associated with the phrase "the ends justify the means." However, psychologists, political scientists, and leadership scholars are among those who believe that some of what Machiavelli had to say was relevant to contemporary leadership and that it was not all evil. While we understand that it may seem rather anti-humanistic to search for any value in what Machiavelli had to say about leadership in *The Prince*, below we attempt to do such.

Machiavelli expounds on how princes build relationships, manage their behavior, and build the potential of people and communities. Here is what he asserts:

- *On the Subject of Relationships.* Princes build a solid foundation of support among people in a community in order to retain their position. If chosen to lead against the will of the people, a person is destined to fail regardless of how good or bad they might be. Enduring princes have the popular support of the community and not just the support of those with power and influence. In fact, one needs to be careful about being too reliant on the power and resources of the few as betrayal is always close by.

  Sometimes supporters outlive their usefulness and must be abandoned. Princes choose friends and supporters wisely as a foe is always in the making. They never stay neutral when friends disagree. Machiavelli warns, "And it will always happen that he who is not your friend will invite you to neutrality, while he who is your friend will call on you to declare yourself openly in arms."[2]

  Princes surround themselves with people who have the capacity and willingness to learn and they avoid the ignorant and arrogant. As quoted, "there are degrees of intelligence, one which understands by itself, a second which understands what is shown it by others, and a third which understands neither by itself nor on the showing of others; the first of which is most excellent, the second is good, but the third is worthless."[2]

  In addition, "the first method for estimating the intelligence of a prince is to look at the men he has around him."[2] Princes are open to the advice and opinions of those who are trusted and wary of flatterers as they will be their undoing.

- *On the Subject of Behavior.* Because it is impossible to possess all of the good behaviors and none of the bad, princes must manage their behavior. Sometimes it is necessary to appear bad or good in order to prevail in a situation – it is the appearance and not the reality that matters. It is noted, "Prudence therefore consists of knowing how to distinguish degrees of disadvantage, and in accepting the less evil as a good."[2]

Machiavelli suggests that the virtues of a prince are what give him the ability to use fortune in his favor. His long-term objectives must be virtuous. If a prince does not have the virtues of good rulers, he should attempt to imitate the virtue of great rulers who have come before him.

Knowing how to manage perception is essential. Princes should not seek to deceive and should not be persuaded by flattery. Any prince "who seeks to deceive will always find someone who will allow himself to be deceived"[2] and that never turns out well in the long run. He also wrote "there is no better way to guard yourself against flattery than by making men understand that telling you the truth will not offend you."[2] He believed openness was essential.

Being seen as generous and sharing the profit of the enterprise builds followers and supporters. There are limits to generosity beyond which the capacity of the organization is impaired. It is far better to be feared than loved, although one would want to be both when possible. Love will be betrayed by self-interests while fear is enduring as leverage because it carries the dread of punishment which is always effective. Being loved depends on how people feel which is fickle; being feared depends on the prince's behavior which can be managed – better to rely on what one can manage than the fickleness of others.

However, there is a boundary between fear and hatred with the latter occurring when people feel overly oppressed. Achievement through the destruction of others may lead to power but it confers no glory. A prince must be feared and respected by the community at large, yet not hated, especially by the people with power and influence. When a prince is hated, they have reason to fear everything and everyone. Machiavelli states, "The best fortress you can have is not being hated by your subjects. If they hate you, no fortress will save you when once the people take up arms."[2]

Thus, a prince must know how to use good and bad behavior discerningly. It is stated, "(be a) fox to discern toils and a lion to drive off wolves." [2] If everyone in the world was good, then this would not be good advice. When people in power are corrupt, one must adapt their behavior to satisfy their needs.

- *On the Subject of Potential.* Princes make the community stronger and viable for the long term and not just the present. They are never lulled into complacency about their security, else they risk the future viability of the organization. They create law and order for the protection of the community while constantly expanding its capacity. Machiavelli states, "Nothing makes a prince so well thought of as to undertake great enterprises and give striking proofs of his capacity."[2]

Good princes create teams of people who manage the work to be done, and reserve only those powers and authority that enhance their grace and favor. They are leery of outsiders (mercenaries), as they weaken the entity's self-sufficiency. Instead, they are constantly building the potential of the members of the community. Those motivated within a community will remain as such as long as they are growing in potential. Machiavelli states, "providing arms to subjects become yours and those who were faithful at first, continue so, and from your subjects become your partisans."[2] Moreover, "A prince should be a patron of merit, and should honor those who excel in every art. He ought to encourage his subjects by enabling them to pursue their callings."[2] As a result, delegation is essential in order to make space for people to act to achieve their responsibilities.

One must be aware of the randomness of the world and maintain an awareness, and act decisively, relative to shifting constraints and opportunities. As stated, "A prince who rests wholly on Fortune is ruined when she changes."[2] Furthermore, "he will prosper most whose mode of acting best adapts itself to the character of the times; and conversely that he will be unprosperous, with whose mode of acting the times do not accord."[2] Thus, a smart prince makes their own luck by interacting with their environments; the inexperienced or unenlightened do not understand this.

The capacity of an organization must be defended against threats. Opponents to the prince must be dealt with decisively, else they will attract the discontented in the community and could lead to an overthrow. Challengers to power are normal and should be expected – it is the avoidance of confrontations by the prince that makes challengers bolder. It is easier to win over hearts and minds through conciliation, so keep those with position and power satiated and the common masses contented. Good will with the community is essential when facing challenges from adversaries. Often, however, opponents must be crushed, and this must be done without destroying the property of the masses in the community.

When capacity is expanded through the acquisition of another organization, the prince must incorporate the acquired quickly and replace the officials of the acquired entity with trusted supporters. Machiavelli states, "He must disarm its inhabitants, except such of them as have taken part with him while he was acquiring it … All arms of the new State shall be in the hands of his own soldiers who have served under him in ancient dominions."[2]

It is important for leaders to have the support of the people. Without support for your decisions, no actions will be successful. The people need to believe in what you are fighting for or they will not join you in battle. If you are not satisfying people's basic needs, they will rebel and kill or banish you.[4]

Much like Machiavelli's proclamations about human nature, it is insightful to ponder if his views about princes are relatable to NELM. We say yes and no. Here is what we think is clearly relatable. He concludes that enduring leaders (we are substituting leaders for princes) build strong relationships within the community, but they are careful with friendships as these can be betrayed.

They choose their inner circle of supporters wisely, and are open to their influence, while they avoid the ignorant and arrogant and those who might manipulate them with flattery – these influences can impair their viability. They see the world as a continuum of constraints and opportunities that must be acted upon. Every challenge must be confronted, else the community will deteriorate. They would prefer to be loved but will accept being feared as that might be the only option in certain times. Above all things, they will avoid being hated as it will be their undoing. Lastly, leaders will defend their positions and the community rigorously. In order to marshal these defenses, it is to their advantage to make the community and its members stronger by supporting their followers. Followers also must believe in the goals and objectives (the future direction) that the leader is espousing. Good leaders also create teams and build the potential of all members of their communities while giving them "space to deliver."

Here is what we think is only partially relatable to NELM. The thought that leaders manage their behavior as a way to influence how they are perceived by the community is entirely consistent with NELM. One should not intentionally deceive but manage impressions to the positive when they have not achieved the skill necessary. Where we cannot agree with Machiavelli is the idea of choosing either good or bad when one or the other is most advantageous, as in meeting corruption in kind and welcoming goodness. This behavior not only conflicts with aspects of ethics and morality in many societies, but it violates the principle of integrity, which we believe is sacrosanct for a leader.

In summary, we believe Machiavelli has some lessons (though couched in 16th century terminology) that can be useful for leaders; his ideas about the ease with which one can countenance violations of integrity are not acceptable.

## Is Godliness Consistent with NELM?

Understanding Machiavellianism was difficult largely because of its complexity and the confusion about Machiavelli's intentions in writing *The Prince*. Godliness is a bit more straight forward.

In order to explore godliness, we needed to define it as a concept which, as we discovered, is not easy to do without creating an affront to faith-based beliefs – which is clearly not our intention. Our starting point was the review of three religions with god as the core of the belief system. These included Christianity, Islam, and Judaism, which collectively represent roughly 55 percent of the world's population.[9] Each religion has a unique context and language of godliness, but a consistent theme is that it is something that is pursued in the present – for the future – with unrelenting and persevering effort., i.e., devotion in action.[5] Godliness is clearly seen as a pattern of behavior supported by congruent attitudes and thinking. It is communal (vs. solely solitary) in that others are either involved in achieving it or are the subject of the godly actions, e.g., Judaism's goal of repairing the world.[6] There is also an aspect of discipline, that begins in the mind, along with the pursuit of training that molds and perfects the character of a person.[7]

Here is the definition of godliness – as a concept – that we concluded from our research:

> It is a discipline of behavior that focuses effort and action on transforming the present state towards perfection. A godly person is on a journey to refine their character, to be self-controlled, trustworthy, and respectable, and to be a role model for the community. They also nurture others' potential without dominating them but by sharing an intense feeling of deep affection.

There are clearly similarities to the profile of a leader that we describe in *Becoming a Leader:*

> Leaders behave in a way that defines success in others' successes, with attention on common goals. Their influence occurs in groups and they meet others' needs. A leader is a role model for others to follow. They initiate and carry the burden of maintaining relationships by being engaged in conversations with people, informing them and seeking their opinion. And lastly, leaders change the way people think about what is possible in the future.

The similarities are even more significant when comparisons[6,8] are made directly to each Element of Leadership Mastery:

- *Setting Direction* among the three religions is a consistent theme, mostly about achieving salvation for self and others by spreading beliefs, striving to serve mankind through passion, justice, trustworthiness, love for all, and doing good deeds.
- *Building the Team* does not have a literal parallel in the religions but is evident in the societal structure of marriage, family, community, and business. Christianity's "12 apostles of Jesus" is clearly aligned with NELM and even has aspects of diversity, e.g., a tax collector, several fisherman, a politician, etc. An example in Islam, the Prophet Muhammad said, "Faithful believers are to each other as the brick of a wall, supporting and reinforcing each other."[10]
- *Creating Key Processes* is readily apparent in Christianity's prescribed sacraments for initiation, healing, and vocation; Judaism's focus on rituals and prayer, and Islam's Five Pillars. There are even echoes of NELM's performance management and rewards in each religion's version of final judgment. For example, in one case final judgment is assessed for a lifetime of efforts to do good and avoid sinful behaviors, deeds, and intentions, and in another it is the ultimate reward of life after death, be it with god or a world to come, and in a third case it is punishment through suffering and torment either for eternity or when god offers deliverance.
- *Stewarding Structure* is evident in the physicality of each religion as well as the assignment of roles, authority, and responsibility. Each has a place

of worship where people congregate, be it a church, mosque, or synagogue. And, each has a body of people with a hierarchy of assigned religious duties. For example, Rabbi, Cantor, and Scribe for Judaism; Bishop, Priest, and Minister for Christianity; and, Iman, Sheikh, and Maulana for Islam.

- *Set Boundaries* that define right and wrong dominate all three religions. These are prescribed by religious laws in scriptures including the Bible, Qur'an, Hadiths, Tanakh, and Torah. In the case of Islam, Shariah Law also extends to business transactions and individual rights, as well as criminal and governmental laws.
- *Nurture Behaviors* has the most compelling parallels to NELM, especially with the concept of managing behavior as an input to what one can be. Much like Machiavelli, each religion is premised on human behavior being self-centered and self-interested. As such, it is accepted that humans are willing to align with good and bad virtues. For Christianity, this willingness is predetermined at birth; Judaism views it as a choice throughout life, while Islam sees it as acquired at the time of puberty. A person works towards good behaviors through sustained daily effort. It requires discipline to deny bad desires and replace them with behavioral patterns that are good. The more this discipline is practiced, the more readily a person acts towards godliness. Being human, perfection is not fully achievable in any of the religions, so disciplined behavior is more about the journey than the destination.[11]
- *Conversations* are featured in each religion and manifested in societal relationships (marriage, etc.) but also in prayer to either saints or God or both. Interestingly, among humans, debate is specifically mentioned in Judaism and Islam and encouraged as part of learning.[6] Through prayer and conversations with others, forgiveness for wrong doings can be sought and achieved.
- *Providing Support* occurs prominently in all three religions, initially through prophets and their works, and also as part of the ongoing role of humans to have love for all and nurture believers and the faithful. Financial support for the community is integral to each of the religions, particularly for Islam, where Zakat, or alms giving and charity, is considered purification and makes the rest of one's wealth legally and religiously pure.[12]
- *Space to Deliver* is inherent to all the religions through the existence of free will. Humans exercise choice over how they live. Direction, structure, process, boundaries, and support are prescribed by the religions, but a person decides to live either a life oriented towards self-interest or a commandment-driven life oriented towards godliness.[11]

Given the definition of godliness and the relatability of three dominant god-based religions to NELM, it is readily apparent that the concept of godliness closely parallels leadership as defined by NELM. (Our impassioned readers and seminar attendees are correct.) Should it be a surprise, really? These religions were documented 1400–3500 years ago by humans. Be they divinely inspired, motivated by observation, or driven to record existing knowledge, what better testament for god is there than that of leadership?

## FINAL WORDS

Is NELM the Holy Grail of leadership? Not sure. But we did illustrate the pervasiveness of NELM in this chapter – it exists in varying degrees in the works of Machiavelli and in the concept of godliness. Perhaps, NELM may be a good fit if we think about the Holy Grail as a goal that is sought after rather than a religious relic that yields eternal life for whoever possesses it. Ultimately, we leave that for you to decide.

## References

1   Adams, S. (2019). *Loserthink*. New York, NY: Penguin.
2   Machiavelli, N. (1513). *The Prince*. Originally published: New York, NY: Collier & Son, c.1910. Edited Edition, Smith, P. (1992) Toronto, Canada: Dover Publications.
3   History.com (n.d.). Retrieved April 6, 2020 from www.history.com/topics/renaissance/machiavelli.
4   Soapboxie (n.d.). Retrieved April 6, 2020 from https://soapboxie.com/social-issues/Characteristics-of-a-Machiavellian-Leader.
5   NavPress (n.d.). What is godliness?. Retrieved March 16, 2020 from https://bible.org/article/what-godliness.
6   Diffen (n.d.). Retrieved March 31, 2020 from https://diffen.com/difference/Islam_vs_Judasim.
7   Pounds, W. (n.d.). Discipline: Train yourself to be godly. Retrieved March 16, 2020 from www.abideinchrist.com/selah/nov25.html.
8   Diffen (n.d.). Retrieved March 31, 2020 from https://diffen.com/difference/Christianity_vs_Islam.
9   Jegede, A. (2019). Top 10 largest religions in the world. Retrieved March 31, 2020 from www.thedailyrecords.com/2018-2019-2020-2021/world-famous-top-10-list/world/largest-religion-in-the-world-fastest-growing/20404/.
10  ezsoftech.com (n.d.). Retrieved March 31, 2020 from www.ezsoftech.com/stories/mis45.asp.
11  Adams, J. (1972). *Godliness through discipline*. Phillipsburgh, NJ: R&R Publishing.
12  ReligionFacts (2017). Islamic beliefs about human nature. ReligionFacts.com, April 9. Retrieved March 29, 2020 from www.religionfacts.com/islam/human-nature.

# 3 MAKING QUALITY DECISIONS

*Being the CEO would be easy if I didn't have to make decisions all of the time.*

That comment was made by one of our coaching clients, the CEO of a package-goods company. He was lamenting about how difficult his world had become, starting about a year earlier, when he was promoted to the CEO of his long-time employer. The 49-year-old bemoaned, "I wanted this job for years – my entire career in fact – and now that I'm here, well, were all of the sacrifices worth it?" He described what he called "being manipulated" by those close to him at work. "I know my VPs are filtering what they say to me ... maybe they're unaware of it or they have their own agendas ... and it always ends up with a decision that falls on me." His issue was not about making decisions, it was about knowing the difference between good and bad input that informs the decision. "It's never black or white ... it's always gray." The worst situations occurred after executive team meetings when difficult issues were discussed. "I walk out of the meeting thinking that I understand what needs to be done, and then come the knocks on my office door ... Do you have a moment to discuss something?" One by one, each of the executives would stop by the CEO's office for a private discussion about insights that just occurred to them or things that were too awkward to discuss in the meeting.

> *By the end of the day, I am angry, confused, and frustrated because I have to make a decision, and it has to be a good quality decision. Making good vs. bad decisions goes with the territory of being a CEO, I know that. But being in a situation where I have to filter through often conflicting perspectives, questionable motivations of my executives, and what emerges as either incomplete information or things that are simply unknowable at the time is, you know, just a huge burden on a steady diet.*

Now, we had many coaching conversations with the CEO about his and the executive team's trust issues, and how his moods and anger can affect his decision-making (see Box 3.1). These conversations also hit on his tolerance of dysfunctional behavior by the executives, and their reluctance to have honest conversations with him that confront issues. We even discussed whether he had made the best career choices. But the issue about making good decisions

DOI: 10.4324/9781003036791-3

in a world loaded with vagaries is not singularly his problem, or one associated with being a CEO; we all deal with the same issue.

We are continuously making decisions whether we realize it or not. Neuroscientists have identified a fascinating dynamic between the subconscious and conscious dimensions of the brain. The subconscious is constantly generating thoughts that appear and disappear without our control. It is like a perpetual churning of random attention to everything that is occurring within and beyond our awareness. This churning generates potentials for action that emerge into our consciousness every .2 seconds.[1] At that point, we decide in the moment to act on the stimulus or not; we actually make a decision, be it driven by reflex or deliberation. Deliberative decisions are the hardest to make because they involve consideration even if it is only momentary. Over a lifetime, a person makes millions of decisions, the quality of which has consequences – that define what we as people become. An accumulation of bad decisions drives a predictable outcome, as will an accumulation of good decisions.

To deal with the persistence and pervasiveness of decision-making, our advice to clients of all ages and stages of careers is to create and sustain their leadership zone.

## Box 3.1: How Moods and Anger Affect Judgment and Decision-Making

### Moods

The effect of moods on judgment has been the subject of a vast amount of psychological research.

"Mood has a measurable influence on what you think: what you notice in your environment, what you retrieve from your memory, and how you make sense of these signals."[2]

Somewhat surprisingly, either a good or bad mood can be beneficial depending on the situation. For example, in negotiations a good mood is advantageous. People in a good mood are more cooperative and elicit more reciprocation. As a result, they tend to have better negotiation outcomes than negotiators who are in a bad mood.

Good moods, however, also make people more gullible. They are less apt to detect deception or identify misleading information. Conversely, eyewitnesses who are exposed to misleading information are better able to disregard it – and to avoid false testimony – when they are in a bad mood.[2]

Mood even influences moral judgments. In a classic moral dilemma, "would you push a man off a bridge to save five people coming across the bridge in a train"? Those who watched a mere five-minute positive video were three times more likely to save the five and kill the man.[2]

In a study by Stanton et al., they found that inducing a happy mood promoted decisions by participants to gamble more compared to those who had a sad or neutral mood induced.[3]

Similarly, Nygren, Isen, Taylor, and Dulin found that participants in positive moods were more likely to overestimate probabilities for winning relative to probabilities for losing while this was not the case for participants in a control condition.[4]

Interestingly, when it comes to information processing, those in more negative moods are more likely to carry out effortful analyses of information while those in positive moods are more likely to rely on peripheral cues. As mood states become more positive, effortful analytic processing of information decreases.[5]

Taken together, in the words of Kahneman, Sibony, and Sunstein "these findings suggest that the moment-to-moment variability of mood affects the quality of our judgments in ways that we cannot possibly hope to control. This variability or 'noise' should give a pause to anyone who thinks he or she can make purely objective judgments. If our mind is a measuring instrument, it is a noisy one."[2]

## Anger

Most that has been written about anger in the workplace has been directed at how to minimize it or deal with it. However, recent research suggests that anger may produce some positive outcomes.

Some of the ways in which anger has been found to be positive are:

- Helping to air differences and facilitate beneficial changes to the status quo. It drives people to adapt and deal with challenges by decreasing aggression, mobilizing energy, and increasing blood flow to muscles.[6] Often important messages are sent that can aid managers in making quality decisions when employees get mad.[7]
- Creating an environment where employees believe they must repress anger and keep it hidden from everyone (silent anger) can result in missed critical information as well as serious physical and psychological health problems for those repressing.[8]
- Muted anger, which is expressed to others but kept from those responsible for triggering it results in no problem solving, and resentment may accelerate over time.[9]
- Intense anger displays from managers can create anxiety in followers which results in greater effort and concentration on the part of employees. (See downsides of intense anger displays below.)[10]
- When leader anger is considered appropriate it can induce guilt which appears to be a healthy emotion that increases effort and helps maintain relationships.[11]
- A manager's high-intensity anger displays may also lead to followers' performance improvement efforts, as they may cause followers to reflect on their own behavior and adjust it accordingly.[12]
- Anger displays by managers can increase perceptions of their prestige and influence.[13]

HOWEVER, there are also serious cautions in expressing anger, particularly for managers and women.

Anger's usefulness in the workplace declines substantially when it is brought to a situation from another source (e.g., fight with spouse at home), affecting people in the moment, and it is unrelated to the issue at hand.[14] While increased work effort on the part of subordinates may lead managers to think their anger is effective it is important to recognize that this enhanced work effort results from followers' feelings of anxiety which may ultimately harm individuals' health.[10] Additionally, higher work effort in reaction to leaders' anger is unlikely to result from their intrinsic motivation; instead, the motivation is to reduce anxiety caused by the anger rather than motivation to work hard. This results in a vicious circle where anger is increasingly needed to motivate, creating a hostile work environment.

Managers who believed their anger expressions were effective were unaware of the broader, longer lasting negative effects such as reduced employee trust, lower satisfaction, and lower morale, all of which are deleterious for long-term performance.[15]

Women need to be particularly cautious in using anger in the workplace because it is viewed as masculine and inconsistent with the expected female gender role. (See "Versatility: A 9th Leadership Behavior" in Chapter 5). Violating stereotypes that women are supposed to be collaborative and conciliatory can trigger harsh judgments when women express anger at work. They are given an "angry woman" label which is unlikely to happen for men.[7]

### Recommendations: Moods and Anger

As leaders we need to be aware that what we think is a "quality decision" on our part may have been shaped by our mood at the time and is a far cry from "quality." This is one of the reasons for the old adage "sleep on it" as you will likely be in a different mood in the morning.

Overall, "research suggests that managers' anger should be used with significant caution while employee anger should be recognized as a potentially valuable signal – a message that managers need to listen to and understand rather than simply reacting defensively or punitively."[7]

Managers need to be curious not furious – never in rage. Try to understand what is behind an employee's anger. "Managers who respond to angry employees with supportiveness and interest can generate positive changes at work; in contrast those who do nothing or choose to penalize angry employees produce no measurable benefits" (Geddes & Stickney, 2011 cited in [7]).

In addition, it is important to provide appropriate space for anger expression. Town halls, soliciting feedback that when negative or angry is listened to, or private meetings with employees to allow them to vent are all constructive ways to keep employees from repressing anger. Repressed anger can inhibit necessary change as well as lead to employee cynicism, resentment, and even hostile outbursts.[7]

## YOUR LEADERSHIP ZONE

In *Becoming a Leader*, we developed the concept of the Leadership Zone by building on research done by Otto Scharmer regarding the pathology of a crisis.[16] When in the leadership zone, one's life is about the avoidance of crises by steering along a journey of successful outcomes. The visual shown in Figure 3.1 is a helpful aid. Imagine that your life is a long driving trip on a desolate road through a broad valley. Out in front of you is a destination that is reachable, with high peaks, but it is not a fixed point; rather it is a broad horizon of possibilities. The road in front of you has wide berms for safe passage and seemingly endless visibility on both sides for opportunities and threats. At any point, you can park the car on the side of the road and venture off on foot in search of new experiences, always returning to the road to continue moving forward into the future. These side trips enrich you by opening your eyes to things that were not visible from the car. In this way you are constantly observing and adapting to the challenges confronted along the road and the

**Figure 3.1** The Journey

opportunities that you encounter. You do not want to go too fast, but you need to keep moving forward. Ultimately, you see the road, the destination, and the valley as a system of interconnected environments and your presence is affecting them, altering them, and redefining your potential. In the end, you realize that a successful outcome is not defined by the destination but rather the quality of the journey.

The journey is driven by the leadership zone – and there are four steps required to be in the zone: (1) be mindful of socialized observations, (2) fracture your ice and the ice of others, (3) detect and confront constraints, and (4) define your relationship with time. These are explained in the following sections. The four steps will put you on a pathway of adapting to – or creating – challenges in what you see as an ever-shifting system of interconnected environments. If you can remain in your leadership zone you will never become what Otto Scharmer describes as:[16]

- *Ignorant:* inwardly focused and consumed with politics and getting buy-in to your agenda. Your perceptions of what is actually going on around you are narrowed to your mental models. Your connection with reality is lost and there is a poor focus on changes occurring in your environment.
- *Arrogant:* your beliefs become so entrenched that they blur your perceptions and blind you to other possibilities. Conflict emerges with people in a fight for whose opinion is correct.

- *Absent:* your self-image drives truths. You cease to be aware of what is going on around you. Your response to challenges, constraints, and opportunities is built on a foundation of preserving your self-image rather than experimentation and observation of what is possible.

## Step 1: Be Mindful of Socialized Observations

I, Al, and my wife, Celeste, were on our first-ever cruise at the time that the House Intelligence Committee began its historic public hearings on the impeachment inquiry of President Trump in 2019. We were both deeply interested in the hearings and were surprised to find that for most of the time on the ship we were in a dead zone for internet and live television coverage. There was cable news available on the television in our room, but it was a day old and only came on late in the afternoon.

For those unfamiliar with cruises, the late afternoon tends to be down time when passengers rest in their rooms after tiring excursions or a day at the pool. It is also a time when it is fairly normal to share a cocktail or two with traveling partners in anticipation of the evening's activities.

Imagine our frustration when, with cocktails in hand, we discovered that only two news networks were offered on the ship: MSNBC, an organization known for its liberal-leaning politics and perceived support of the Democratic Party, and FOX NEWS, an organization known for its conservative-leaning politics and perceived support of the Republican Party. It was astonishing to listen to a FOX NEWS anchor report on an event that occurred in the hearings as profound evidence that President Trump is a victim of conspiracy, and then flip the station to MSNBC and hear the same event described as equally profound evidence that President Trump is a villain. Political divisiveness, i.e., victim or villain and nothing in between, that is what we were left with over cocktails.

Unable to view the actual hearings, we could not form our own opinions, rather we had to filter through (1) the motivations and (2) the biases of the networks and their anchors in order to determine what actually occurred. Celeste asked, "Which one of them is lying?" I responded, "It depends on the context that you bring to the situation." She replied, "Come on Al; can't you park the leadership stuff while we're on vacation?" That hurt a little. *(Truth is – I try to be in my leadership zone 100 percent of the time.)*

As to context, let us start first with the motivation of the networks. It is important to remember that both networks are commercial enterprises. Meaning, they are motivated to make money. They have owners and shareholders who want an economic return on their investment. Each network seeks distinctiveness, in an extremely competitive market, in order to attract advertisers who pay for commercials, and for subscription revenue from other cable and streaming companies. They gain this distinctiveness by creating a brand image that draws and retains viewers. The brand also attracts employees and other investors who subscribe to the values represented by the brand. Over time these employees become managers in their companies and the brand values become intertwined into a persona, if not a social role as an "ideological force for good" for the viewers, employees, managers, and investors whose beliefs align with the brand values.

Bottom line: in today's extremely competitive market for reporting "the news," it is good business for news-media companies to be branded as either conservative- or liberal-leaning. And once the brand is established, compromising it by reporting news that conflicts with the brand identity is bad business. Prior to internet-driven social media, balanced news reporting was a profitable business. That business model was displaced when digital technology advanced to the point that media companies could measure which content attracted and influenced the most viewership – and thus made it possible to measure the profitability of different approaches to reporting news.[42] Now there are hundreds if not thousands of sources of news on cable stations, network stations, and the internet – having a distinctive brand identity is essential for survival.

You might think at this point that we are suggesting that the media intentionally misrepresent the news. Surely the executives of these companies assert that they provide balanced editorial content, and they believe as such. That brings us to the second aspect of context, biases.

As co-authors we have written extensively about how observations shape reality. Our brains create mental models from a lifetime of observations which subconsciously drive our beliefs and decision-making. As a result, truth and reality are subjective, and have a lot to do with how, where, and with whom we lived our lives up to that point in time. For example, if a person only watches FOX NEWS, the reporting of that network will over time become socialized in the person and among those others within their network of relationships. The same occurs for someone who only watches MSNBC. This socialization has an organic personification – it is like a pandemic of biases.

The granddaddy of all biases is called Cognitive Dissonance (see Box 3.2 Theory of Cognitive Dissonance). It is theorized that a person will experience stress if they hold contradictory beliefs, ideas, or values, which is not sustainable for healthy mental functioning. Unconsciously, they will eliminate contradictory information (observations) or reframe it in order to achieve internal congruence. This reframing can extend to their own actions as the brain strives for self-justification.

## Box 3.2: Theory of Cognitive Dissonance

The theory of cognitive dissonance was initially proposed by psychologist Leon Festinger in his book *A Theory of Cognitive Dissonance*, published in 1957.[17] "Cognitive dissonance has been one of the most enduring and successful theories in the history of social psychology."[48] This theory proposes that people are averse to inconsistencies within their own minds. It provides a reason why people adjust their thinking or behavior when they are not aligned. When people's cognitions are inconsistent, they experience psychological discomfort[49] and unpleasant physiological states of stress are activated.[50]

Inconsistencies make us feel uncomfortable, so we try to resolve them. Festinger saw cognitive dissonance as a motivator for individuals to change either their thinking or behavior to reduce dissonance. For example when we hear new information that challenges what we believe, we may choose to ignore it or disbelieve it. Or, for example, if a woman tells a lie and feels uncomfortable about it because her self-image is one of an honest person, she is experiencing cognitive dissonance between how she sees herself and how she behaved. Though a person may not always resolve cognitive dissonance, the responses to it may range from discounting the source or the information to changing one's beliefs or behavior to eliminate the conflict.

Unfortunately, many of the reactions to dissonance are not part of good leadership. For example, one way to avoid the negative outcomes of cognitive dissonance is to avoid situations or information that create inner conflict.[51] This is problematic and creates hierarchy myopia – possibly ignoring very pertinent information necessary for good decision-making. Additionally, research has shown that when an individual receives information that is inconsistent with his or her beliefs, he or she will seek out information that confirms what they want to believe.[52] Another leadership example of the problem of dissonance is when leaders fail to acknowledge weaknesses because they are not consistent with their ideal self-view. As such, they do not acknowledge or address these weaknesses.

Self-awareness is one key to understanding how and when cognitive dissonance may be operating in your thinking. If you find yourself justifying or rationalizing decisions or behaviors that you are not quite clear you firmly believe in, that might be a sign that cognitive dissonance is at work. Try to avoid the temptation to rationalize and to seek confirming information. Force yourself to ask, "could I be wrong"?

The more a person or community has riding on a judgment, the more likely they are to unconsciously manipulate, attend to, or ignore information. For example, during the COVID-19 pandemic, which began in earnest in the US in early 2020 and was under way as of this writing, many state governors ordered people to stay at home and businesses to close their doors in order to avoid the spread of the nasty virus which had no cure or vaccine. People had quite different reactions to these stay-at-home orders. Some believed they were extremely prudent, others thought they were a gross over-reaction, and others were convinced they were a violation of human rights. One noted politician, Dan Patrick of Texas, went so far as to say "there are more important things than living. And that's saving this country for my children and my grandchildren and saving this country for all of us … we've got to take some risks and get back in the game and get this country back up and running."[18] The position any individual took on the issue was highly influenced by the factors we mentioned earlier. Who were they listening to among the many contradictory voices? What information did they choose to ignore or reframe and why? What was at stake for them personally (e.g., family situation, personal health, financial situation)? What were their values, ideologies, and political beliefs?

Another example is the rapid rise and tremendous fall of businesswoman Elizabeth Holmes. Her now-defunct startup, Theranos, was a unicorn among venture capitalists and soared in market value to $9 billion[25] in 2015, based on reported breakthroughs in blood-testing technology. Her emerging reputation as a young, brilliant innovator attracted money and support of influential people from high-profile political, military, and business backgrounds who were aligned with the image that she represented.[26] The lead product – a portable blood analyzer – was installed by retail chains and over a million blood assessments were conducted. In 2018, the U.S. Security and Exchange Commission charged Theranos and Holmes with a "years-long fraud in which they exaggerated or made false statement about the company's (blood-testing) technology, business, and financial performance … involving $700 million raised from investors."[27] Holms settled with the SEC by agreeing to be stripped of control of the company, barred from serving as an officer or director of a public company, and payment of a $500,000 penalty. Subsequently, a federal grand jury indicted Holmes on multiple counts of wire fraud and conspiracy for distributing blood tests with falsified results to consumers.[28]

The scale of the alleged fraud and the pedigree of the Theranos investors and business partners raise similar questions as noted above about COVID-19. These examples illustrate that each of us is prone to self-justification through cognitive dissonance, meaning that our observations can be selective and, even then, we can unconsciously reframe them to fit our political, ideological, or value-based beliefs. Moreover, we socialize the observations of others including what is reported to us through whatever media outlets we frequent. As noted above, these media outlets are influenced by profitability goals and the motivations and cognitive dissonance of their owners, managers, and employees. If we are not mindful of these socialized observations, the likelihood of becoming ignorant, arrogant, or absent (i.e., outside a viable leadership zone) is quite high.

We also need to be mindful of algorithms utilized by online social networks like Facebook, Google, YouTube, Twitter, LinkedIn, and Instagram.[38,39,40] Algorithms are automated calculations, imperceptible by users, created by social media companies to feed paid advertisements and free content to users based on what they have shown interest in. Content is prioritized based on the extent of the user's online engagement with specific friends, family members, online purchases, videos watched, sites they have clicked on, and content searches they have made in the past. As a result, the algorithms can create an "echo chamber" where users see prioritized content from like-minded people and online media sources.[19] Although dissonance is reduced by the algorithms, they tend to create gradual, slight, and imperceptible changes in the user's behavior and perception,[44] in what can become a "cocoon" supported by the following cognitive and social biases:

- *The Recency Bias* – we think that whatever we heard or read about most recently is more common or more important than it actually is, making our judgments and opinions biased toward the latest news or information.[54]
- *The Availability Bias* – our tendency to think whatever is easily recalled or comes to mind quickly is more important than it actually is.

- *The Extremity Bias* – we share (as do others) the most extreme version of any story, making a positive story glowing and a negative one horrific. Our tendency is to think that extreme things that come readily to mind are more common or important than they really are. We overestimate the probability of events associated with memorable or vivid events. For example if you saw someone get struck by lightning (actual probability is 1 in 600,000) you believe the risk is much greater. Research findings about social media have shown that user-generated content portrays behavior that is more extreme than what is observed offline and in non-media contexts.[20,21]
- *The Confirmation Bias* – we observe information that confirms our pre-existing views and ignore information that does not. This bias is exacerbated in social media when people are bucketed and fed information that conforms to whatever they have searched for in the past, creating polarized communities with divergent views of reality.[20]

Think about this complex question? In a world where we are (1) driven by self-justification, (2) cocooned by a plethora of cognitive and social biases into communities of divergent realities, and (3) influenced by imperceptible algorithms created by commercially driven social media companies, is it possible to have a viable leadership zone? Moreover, as lamented by the CEO at the beginning of this chapter, can we ever make quality decisions? Yes, is the answer to both questions – but it takes effort. The first step is to give yourself permission to be aware of how socialized observations are affecting your version of reality. For many, this first step is the hardest.

## Step 2: Fracture Your Ice and the Ice of Others

I, Al, live on an island in Alaska. It can be a challenging lifestyle, especially in the winter when the ice is not fully formed. I wait for at least 11 inches of ice before driving my pickup truck across the frozen lake, but I will walk over with as little as 3 or 4 inches of thickness. Last December, my wife and I were walking the 1 mile distance over clear ice (meaning we could see the water under the ice) to the house, and we were alarmed (frightened more like it) by the sound of "popping" all around us, including the sound that seemed to be coming from hundreds of yards ahead of us. Once safely in the house, my curiosity led to some online research; I was intrigued by what I learned. When ice forms, it creates a perfect equilibrium of tension, meaning the tension is what keeps the ice in a steady state. Any external influence (e.g., my wife and I walking on it) will disturb the equilibrium and cause a break in the tension. Depending on the thickness, a fracture in the ice might occur. These fractures could go through the entire depth of the ice and appear at great distances from where the external influence occurred. So, my 230 pounds could fracture the ice not only around me but miles away on the other side of the lake. When a fracture refreezes, it is actually stronger than the original ice. This means the more that ice is fractured in a consistently low temperature environment, the stronger and more viable it becomes to withstand even greater external influences. Most people think of ice as rigid and unforgiving, and crossing it as dangerous, but it actually is not.

We will explain how this rather amazing insight has implications for a person's ability to sustain their leadership zone in the wake of cognitive dissonance, biases associated with socialized observations, and the ever-changing landscape of context. But first we need to develop some helpful context. To do so we are going to use some perspectives from Annie Duke's *Thinking in Bets*[22] and Matthew Syed's *Black Box Thinking*.[23]

Annie Duke is a former professional poker player turned author and consultant. She asserts that a person's life is similar to a poker hand in that it involves seeing possible choices, making decisions, luck, and uncertainty. She goes on to say that creating successful outcomes, i.e., quality decisions, in any situation requires three things:

- A willingness and ability to consider facts, knowledge, and what we believe, as well as having a mechanism to constantly challenge each.
- Accepting that luck exists and acknowledging the randomness of factors and influences in our lives. This allows us to be free of what psychologists call a "self-serving bias" whereby we blame our own bad outcomes on either luck or someone else and good outcomes on skillful decision-making. Without this acknowledgment, she argues that we will never examine our decision-making process for errors, which will cause us to miss future opportunities. Stated alternatively, acknowledging the randomness in life allows us to be able to constantly refine our decision-making process.
- Anticipating that there is always unawareness or hidden information at the time of decision-making, and further complications can emerge from unknown future information and factors. She believes that the world does not easily reveal the objective truth in anything. Moreover, "the influence of hidden information on top of luck makes happiness (successful outcomes) difficult to achieve."[22]

To Annie's triad we will add Matthew Syed's focus on "error signals" in the process of making decisions.[23] Leaders need to socialize a mindset of knowing and sharing learning from mistakes. They do this by accepting that errors are made, and they face up to failures. "We cannot learn if we close our eyes to inconvenient truths."[23] Leaders do not punish those who make mistakes, or focus on assigning fault; else, over time the value of mistakes – learning – will be lost and the decision-making process will not improve.

Interestingly, both Annie and Matthew suggest that decision-makers need to have a trigger mechanism that causes them to take inventory of the evidence that informed their facts, knowledge, or beliefs. The act of "taking inventory" could be as simple as asking, "How do I know this?" or as challenging as assessing the credibility of the source that provided the information.

Annie takes it one step further with her belief that decision-makers need to communicate uncertainty to others in a way that invites them to collaborate in the decision-making process. For example, when a person declares something as 100 percent factual, it makes others reluctant to challenge them. On the other hand, when they communicate uncertainty (e.g., "I'm not sure") as they share beliefs, they are implicitly inviting others to help them refine their beliefs. She says, "We are inviting the people in our lives to act like scientists with us."[22] This is not always easy because leaders may feel that admitting uncertainty will be perceived as a weakness. Instead it allows others to feel valued for their ideas and contributions and shows humility (a valued leader trait).

So, let us now go back to the journey over the ice. We believe that people who allow their "ice to be fractured" (metaphorically) have a higher occurrence of successful outcomes in their life. Such people use others as collaborators – the trigger mechanism – in a way that fractures the equilibrium (cocoon of biases) that they have created for themselves in their state of knowledge, facts, ideology, and beliefs. And the more often they do this the better will be the outcome from their decision-making. It is as noted by songwriter Leonard Cohen, in the song "Anthem." [41] He asserts that people need to forget what they consider perfect and allow their world to be "cracked" – that is how the new light of wisdom gets in.

In *Becoming a Leader* we explained that great leaders do not fall prey to their own mental models – they intentionally nurture challenge for themselves and others by creating "violations"[37] that break mindsets, "let the light in," and awaken an awareness of constantly changing realities. This awakening creates openness to possibilities that otherwise would not be observed.

To create these violations, which we are now going to call "fractures," we use a technique borrowed from conversations guru Susan Scott, called "Interrogating Reality." [24] It is a style of interaction with people that involves the following:

- *Make a Proposal*. Leaders do not declare their version of truth. Instead, they fashion their interventions with people as proposals that could be right or wrong. A simple sentence structure is as follows: This is the issue, and this is what I am thinking about it. By adding uncertainty to a statement we invite others to challenge us. Merely saying, "This is what I believe, but I'm not sure" encourages others to share their version of truth with us. The more fractures that occur in our state of knowledge and beliefs system, the more often they "refreeze," and the stronger our decision-making quality becomes. The same applies to those involved in the conversation and anyone else socialized in their network. Everyone learns when "facts" are interrogated rather than accepted as truth. Extending the ice metaphor, "the fractures do not only occur around us but develop miles away on the other side of the lake."
- *Check for Understanding*. Leaders intentionally invite people to share their views about a proposal and they make sure that everyone involved gets a chance to speak. This is the heart of the trigger mechanism that causes people to challenge why or how they know something. It is critical for

the leader to resist the tendency to defend his or her ideas. That would shut down the very openness to possibilities that a proposal encourages (see Box 3.3 The Dangers of Defensiveness). Imagine if the managers at Boeing would have invited more input from their engineers and technicians. The 737 MAX disasters may have been diverted.

- *Check for Agreement.* Once the understanding of a proposal has been established, a leader then brings closure to the interrogation by summarizing the various options and sharing his or her view of what has been learned. This is where Annie Duke's "scientists" and Matthew Syed's "error signals" emerge. If the right people are involved, insights fall out from the conversation that inform the decision. If a decision does not occur, then the leader will make it, but still invite others to create more fractures by stating something like, "I believe this is the right way to go, but I suspect some of you might see it differently, so please speak up."

We now have a way for a person to create fractures that let in the light to sustain a leadership zone and improve the ability to make quality decisions along life's journey. The next challenge we will cover is how to enhance the journey by detecting and confronting constraints, in this way uncovering hidden information and opportunities.

## Box 3.3: The Dangers of Defensiveness

A classic experiment was done with chickens trying to increase their egg production.[53] In the chicken business star performers are those who lay the most eggs. Interestingly, they become star performers because they attack the other chickens. Modest performers in the chicken world produce fewer eggs, but they are less aggressive.

A farmer conducted an experiment to breed the most productive star performing chickens. He bred the star performers (red zone chickens) with other star performers and the modest performers (green zone chickens) with other modest performers for a year. In the chicken experiment after one year, half of the star performers had been murdered by their colleagues (obviously production from the group was low) while the modest performers who got along had their production increase by 260 percent (likely because they did not have to deal with the star performers).[53]

We can think of these star performers and those who are not stars but get along with others in our own workplaces. Red zone environments create competition and aggressive behavior while green environments emphasize cooperation and collaboration. Green environments end up being healthier and more productive (they produce more "eggs") in the long run.

Jim Tamm (see link below) mediated labor disputes for years in California. They all quickly turned into red zone environments. So, he decided to start training each side in collaboration. And it worked.

His approach is described below. Basically he contends that red zone behavior is driven by defensiveness which is shaped by the fear of being vulnerable. We fear that our competence, significance, or likeability is being threatened. We are defending ourselves not from others, but from fears we do not want to face. When we become defensive, we become rigid and make poor decisions and promote more defensiveness among others.

When someone pushes our button … then the button pusher owns us. We do not even recognize we are getting defensive until it is too late. So, a great way to improve your ability to solve problems and increase your effectiveness is to manage your own defensiveness with the following actions:[53]

*#1:* Acknowledge it. Recognize that everyone is going to get defensive at times.

*#2:* Try to identify your triggers. What pushes your button and how do you react to it? In order to stop defensiveness in its tracks, you have to identify its first signs (for you). You need an early warning system that you are heading down that path … some possibilities might be:

- Needing to have the last word
- Blaming others
- Wanting to be right
- Withdrawing into deadly silence
- Obsessive thinking
- All or nothing thinking
- Pulse rate increases
- Putting others down
- Exaggerating to make your point
- Thinking only of what you are going to say or do next
- Becoming argumentative
- Breathing gets faster
- You start talking louder
- You feel like you are not being paid attention.

*#3:* Slow down your physiology … whatever works for you … deep breaths, take a walk, tune out.

*#4:* Be aware of your self-talk … are you awfulizing or blowing things out of proportion?

*#5:* Create an action step related directly to your sign of defensiveness.

- If you become argumentative, just stop talking for a few minutes.
- If you start talking louder, consciously take it down a notch.

*#6:* Let it go and start over.

*#7:* Practice your action steps when the stakes are low so you can use them when the stakes are higher.

If you can control your defensiveness, you will be much better at collaboration and problem solving and less aggressive/angry and confrontational.

See this TED talk by Jim Tamm for a complete description. www.ted.com/talks/ jim_tamm_first_step_to_collaboration_don_t_be_so_defensive#t-766008

## Step 3: Detect and Confront Constraints

We have coached a lot of clients over the years. Each is on a unique journey – on their version of the road shown in Figure 3.1. Some clients drive so fast that the journey becomes a blur and they miss what is occurring as they speed past environments. Or, they are so afraid to make a wrong turn that they never achieve their fullest potential. Others seem to ground themselves in the moment, perceiving threats, and opportunities, and constantly adapting to shifts in the environment along the road – some of which their presence created. Among our clients, those who appreciate the singularity of "the moment" have consistently progressed further than those who do not. We will explain this last thought.

There is an emotional scene in the movie *Peaceful Warrior* when a spiritual guide, portrayed by actor Nick Nolte, advises a troubled young gymnast named Dan. (The movie is based on the novel *The Way of the Peaceful Warrior* by Dan Millman who is attributed with the quote "There are no ordinary moments." [29]) In an emotional scene the guide exclaims to Dan that he needs to clear his mind euphemistically by "taking out the trash."[30] The trash is anything and everything that stops a person from being fully present in the moment. The guide goes on to assert that one's full potential is achieved by being in the here and now of the moment.

The point is that our environments are not static, i.e., "There's never nothing going on." They are constantly changing, and our perception of change is stymied by our capacity to observe. It is not enough to be mindful of socialized observations and fracturing ice, we need to be able to observe and understand the implications of a near-constant change in the environments. Without the latter we will be left with "trash," i.e., complacency about threats, constraints, and opportunities. Imagine, for example, if someone would have detected back in November 2019 the singular moment when the COVID-19 virus first transferred from whatever origin to a human.[31] Imagine further if that person would have had the foresight to contemplate the implications of the transfer, then to anticipate the need to respond promptly to the threat, and finally cause authorities to implement processes and procedures to confront the challenge. Consider the cost of this singular moment that went undetected: 585,000 virus-related deaths in the US and 3,274,000 worldwide, unknowable social and health issues due to protracted distress and panic, and devastated economies across the globe with record job losses – 25 million in the US alone.[32,33]

Could all of this have been avoided? Of course. Before explaining how, we want to share one more piece of context about relationships.

We have explained the need to fracture ice (explore, fail, strengthen) as a trigger mechanism to cause us to take inventory of *what we know* – as well as how we know it. Given the randomness of influences in our lives we also need a trigger mechanism for the domain of *what we do not know*. Much of what occurs along our life's journey will be threats and opportunities that are hidden to us because we do not know that they exist. As explained in *Becoming a Leader*, the trigger mechanism for awareness is a rigorous and purposeful relationship with the environments that influence our existence. "Nothing happens in the world without something or someone encountering something else." [34] We are constantly "creating the world" as we participate and collaborate in relationship-related encounters. These could be relationships with family members, managers, business partners, customers, industry competitors, etc. It also could be relationships with those things and people that influence technology and innovation (see Chapter 7). The greater the breadth and depth of relationships with these environments, the greater is our ability to under-stand them and our influence over them. Much of what is unknowable to us is simply a result of shallow relationships in our key environments; we are not observing, listening, exploring, acting, failing, succeeding, learning …

With that context now clear, the "tip of the sword" that we advocate for awareness of threats and opportunities is the identification and acknowledg-ment of constraints that environments impose on our potential. The flip side of a constraint is almost always an opportunity. This opportunity emerges as decision-driven action – to either mitigate or eliminate a threat or capture a breakthrough. Thus the trigger mechanism is twofold: (1) possessing broad and deep environment-relationships and (2) identifying and acknowledging constraints.

We have seen this trigger mechanism occur in recent corporate actions. For example, BP, a leading global producer of oil and gas, has embraced the con-straint of climate change (on its long-term viability) and embarked on a series of strategic actions to transform the company to achieve zero carbon emissions by 2050.[45] Tesla Motors continues to embrace the constraints imposed by bat-tery technology with an objective to create cost-effective all-electric vehicles with the capacity to go 400 miles or more between charges and lasting as long as 1 million miles.[46] And, Advanced Micro Devices (AMD), long a laggard behind Intel in the semiconductor industry, achieved a substantial turnaround by unshackling itself from the constraints of the desktop computing market and shifting into markets for specialized chips for graphics processors and gaming consoles.[47]

In consulting with companies over the years we have facilitated man-agement teams in environment-relationship reviews that have identified con-straints. As an example of the output from these reviews, Figure 3.2 is a list of environmental constraints identified for our client, the CEO of the pack-age-goods company mentioned at the beginning of this chapter. These con-straints are centered in the following categories: processes, culture/structure, people-related, and external.

Once environmental constraints are identified, opportunities for action will emerge. Figure 3.3 provides an example of prioritized actions that the CEO's management team created in reaction to the identification of the constraints.

A comparison of Figures 3.2 and 3.3 might suggest that the two are dis-connected. This illustrates how the detection of constraints can lead to actions that often appear unrelated or tangential to the constraints. But a closer exam-ination of the two reveals the alignment. For example, *recruit experts* and *develop mentoring*, and *internship programs* are in response to *inadequate talent development, employee skill gaps, ageing workforce*, and *retention issues. Set goals, improve performance management, CEO steps back*, and *develop an authority matrix* are in response to *insufficient authority delegated, planning too centralized*, and *weak accountability*. These actions and others were hidden from the manage-ment team's consciousness – the awareness of the constraints illuminated the need for actions.

This is a powerful and often unexpected outcome that can occur from the sequence of thinking through environment-relationships > constraints > actions. When implemented, the actions caused our client initially to adapt to its environments. That adaption affected change in these environments

**External**
- "Green" and renewable preferences
- Emerging competitors
- New and onerous regulations
- Adverse local and national politics
- Weakening economy/demand
- Over-reach by investors into management's role
- Scarcity of critical resources

**Processes**
- Poor management of change
- Inadequate communication
- Lack of internal coordination
- Inconsistent decision-making
- Planning process too centralized
- Slow take-up of new technology
- Insufficient authority delegated relative to responsibility

**People-Related**
- Weak accountability
- Lack of ownership among employees
- Employee skill gaps
- Inadequate talent development
- Poor knowledge transfer
- Ageing workforce – loss of experience
- Pervasive lack of trust
- Employee retention issues

**Culture/Structural**
- Organizational silos
- Employees treated as commodities rather than resources
- Fear of failure
- Management disconnected for operational realities
- Too short-term focused
- Lack of shared values

**Figure 3.2** Environmental Constraints in a Consumer-Packaged Goods Company

**Top Improvement Actions**
- Develop clear vision about diversification and dedicate resources to get there
- Recruit experts for the business lines we want to grow
- Change business line thinking: (1) better balance cost recovery with external realities and (2) look for more high-margin markets
- Set goals, improve performance management, and CEO steps back and monitors

**Critical To Do**
- Formalize the decision-making process
- Incorporate leadership skills into the executive team and make unproductive behaviors unacceptable
- Improve messaging, i.e., communicate expectations and involve employees more in the process

**Highly Important**
- Divest poor performing investments
- Enhance profitable lines
- Develop mechanism and structure to deploy capital
- Restructure debt to maximize cash for growth
- Create mentoring and internship programs
- Develop an authority delegation matrix

**Moderately Important**
- Develop marketing strategy to enhance image
- Develop and distribute on-boarding materials that explain vision and goals
- CEO and executives "get their hands duty" i.e., spend more time in the field
- Integrate new business values with our traditional corporate culture

**Figure 3.3** Prioritized Actions "Triggered" by the Identification of Constraints

as competitors did or did not detect – in a singular moment – and react to our client's influence. When detected by the competitors, our client's actions occurred to them as a new constraint. Hence, a dynamic shifting of environments occurred, and still does in perpetuity, with my client and its competitors not only adapting to but causing change. Those companies that perceive the shifts will progress; those that do not will decline.

Authors Ronald Heifetz and Marty Linsky have written extensively about the evolutionary impact of adaptability: "an essential ingredient for surviving and thriving for every species of life, from life's beginning on earth."[35] They argue all human systems face challenges and must adapt in a world of uncertainty and change, be they "global networks, a nation, a tribe, a town, a company, a family, or a person."[35]

The conceptual framework that we advance to clients is illustrated in Figure 3.4. In the short term, we either do (Yes) or do not (No) detect constraints in our environments that can occur randomly "in the moment." If yes, we are in a position to confront the constraint through some deliberate action. If no, we begin a progression of decline and ultimately end in failure. For example, the CEO of the consumer products company *detected constraints* and *confronted* them by changing the business line thinking, divesting some poor performing investments, and shifting into more profitable lines. When the environment reacted to our client's actions, he *responded* to this feedback with further actions, and ultimately, he *adapted* to the shifting environment

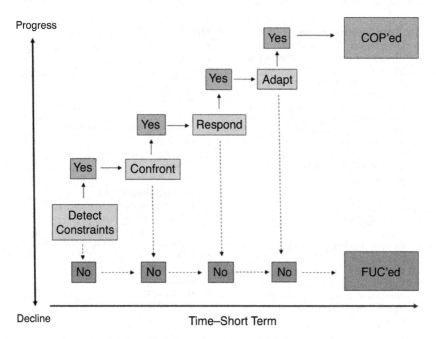

**Figure 3.4** Short-term identification of environmental constraints

that he influenced. In this pattern, the detection sets forth actions that *create opportunities* to *progress*, or COP'ed for short. In the opposite pattern (No), entities do not keep pace with shifting environments, and that leads to *failure, underperformance*, or *crisis*, or FUC'ed for short. (Excuse our fun with acronyms.)

In the long-term, environments are constantly shifting, affected by many factors in addition to our actions. As a result we are in a perpetual state of detection > confrontation > response > adaptation. The rigor of the relationship with the environment, or lack thereof, is pervasive throughout COP'ed and FUC'ed long-term patterns. This relationship is critical for constraint detection but also for the feedback loop as the environment reacts.

Did you notice the other critical component of the COP'ed pattern? We have written about it exhaustively – confrontation. Detection of a constraint goes nowhere without a confrontation. Being *mindful of socialized observations* and *fracturing ice* also require confrontations, be they about biases, taking inventory of evidence, or mental models. We also saw the same in Chapter 1 with the Veritas Conversation in dealing with disputes and disagreements and in Chapter 2 with Machiavelli's advice about challengers to power. As we paraphrased Machiavelli: Challengers are normal and should be expected – it is the avoidance of confrontations that makes challengers bolder … opponents must be crushed (not our words), and this must be done without destroying the property of the masses in the community.

Confrontation is, in fact, a major stumbling block among all of the clients we have coached over the years. It takes courage to confront constraints. It can be tempting to "let it ride" hoping that a constraint will dissolve on its own, never acknowledging (cognitive dissonance) that an opportunity may have been missed had the constraint been addressed. There is always some fear of failure when a person acts to address a constraint. We coach our clients to "back into" courage by considering the regrets of not acting. We remind them that every .2 seconds they are actually making a decision, be it reflexive or deliberative, and non-action is a decision by default. How bad could it get? What will be lost? We actually use Figure 3.4 to help clients overcome courage issues.

So, let us go back to the question about the COVID-19 pandemic: could it have been avoided? The answer is yes, had the relationship, or series of relationships, between the origin of the virus and the first infected human been rigorous enough for the transference to have been detected, and had the people involved operated with the courage to confront the issue with decisive and timely actions.

Appropriately, this insight brings us to the fourth and final step in creating and sustaining a leadership zone: define your relationship with time.

## Step 4: Define Your Relationship with Time

In keeping with the COVID-19 theme which, as noted earlier, was an active crisis at the time of this writing, an immunologist cautioned during a televised press briefing, "It's going to take time to identify and properly test a vaccine." When I, Al, saw this, an image of Mick Jagger singing "Time Is on My Side" instantly popped into my mind and I could not let it go. No matter what I was doing, working in my office, riding my bike, or watching television, the chorus of the song kept playing in the background.

It is an old song, but it is surprising to learn that it was recorded 56 years ago. The shock is really about age, as some of us are old enough to remember watching the Rolling Stones perform the song on the Ed Sullivan show. Isn't it amazing how the passage of time can catch us off guard?

The song has nothing to do with a viral contagion, rather it describes a loving relationship between two people that is falling apart. One person in the relationship wants to be free and the other person is reluctantly letting them go, but with the confidence that – *in time* – they will come running back to them.

Throughout the COVID-19 crisis many people lost something or someone – and they wanted "to go running back" to where they were before the crisis. We saw, experienced, or read about a tsunami of job losses, economies collapsing, and the passing of loved ones. Uncertainty about a cure, a vaccine, and an ending point to the crisis was a source of never-ending stress.

We also experienced some level of disruption in our "normal" time through quarantining or stay-at-home orders. One way or another we all adapted to the constraints imposed by the virus. Some people found opportunities – *more time* – for example, in the elimination of travel to and from work. This time was reallocated to homeschooling children, jogging in the middle of the day, or re-discovering a passion for reading books.

The pattern of time is so ingrained in human consciousness that its passage is taken for granted (like noted with the Rolling Stones' song). For example, the eight-hour workday shifted for white-collar Americans during the crisis. A routine of working four hours, eating lunch, and working another four hours was replaced by ad hoc patterns. Work time occurred more variably, with some people in back-to-back video conference meetings all day, and others with a lot of free time on their hands. Lunch did not occur at a set time; it was replaced by a chance moment when one was near the refrigerator. People stayed up longer and slept later and often more hours each night. One of our clients commented that "I have so much time that I can't get anything done … I was way more productive when I had less time to do things." Another client stated that balancing the time for work and looking after the children was a persistent tension.

Our hope throughout the crisis was – *it is just a matter of time* – that is, that someone would find a vaccine. *Time is on our side* – that has been our unspoken and perhaps unacknowledged belief.

It is amazing how the word "time" and its reality feature so pervasively in our leadership zone, yet our relationship with time is often unclear. The visual of the highway shown at the beginning of this chapter is actually an image of the passing of time with the past behind us and the future someplace down the road. It is meant to be an aid in imagining the future, which is heavily dependent on how we see the present. The reality is that time is difficult to think and reason about because it is an abstraction, i.e., it is a concept rather than an object.[43] "It cannot be poke, peeled, prodded, pushed, painted, or pierced"[43] Thus, we need a visual – in this case a highway – to make time real for us. Our journey is the passing of time.

A friend recommended a little book to read, *Leonardo and Gabriel*, by Tim Tigner. The book is all about time, and how influential it is in our lives. Provocatively, and with an Einsteinian flair, Tigner takes us through a fictional conversation between Leonardo Di Vinci and the angel Gabriel that concludes that (1) there is nothing without time, (2) there is nothing more powerful than time, and (3) there is nothing left in the world if you take away time. He notes that it is often said, "Time judges all things and only time will tell."[36] In fact, "Judgement is stored in time and transmitted by people through their works, words, memories, and emotions."[36] Time bears witness to everything and it heals all wounds.

The most profound point in the book is that "every minute of time is a gift."[36] He explains that the elderly worship youth for this reason. Young children, on the other hand, do not realize that they are (and feel) vibrant and free because they have plenty of time. (We strongly suggest that our readers also read *Leonardo and Gabriel* in order to fully embrace the messages.)

Perhaps one of the important takeaways from the COVID-19 experience is that time may be on our side, but we must spend it well. Leaders must be decisive, and they must communicate how decisions are made in order to gain support in an organization. If we delay action, it has a cost. It can invite failure or force our hand into less optimal outcomes. If we act too soon, we could go down the wrong path. Time will judge leaders based on how they use – time.

We need to stay focused on our use of time while moving forward on our journey; never too fast or too slow. There is nothing more gratifying than time well spent and nothing worse than the loss of opportunity because of a poor use of time. Each moment (.2 seconds) matters and we need to treat time with the respect that it is due. We are leaders when we use time – to do in the singularity of the moment – what will make us, our families, and our organizations healthier tomorrow.

## FINAL WORDS

We started this chapter with a CEO's grief about wanting to make quality decisions when he had to deal with a steady diet of incomplete or otherwise dubious information. We are pleased to report that the CEO eventually became less tolerant of his executive team's dysfunctional behavior. He not only confronted them, but he confronted the environmental constraints to his company's future. His company is now a top-tier competitor in its industry.

As we discovered, the CEO's problem is not unique to people with lofty executive titles; each of us deals with the same issue throughout our lives. We are constantly making decisions, reflexively or deliberatively, and influenced by moods and anger, that define what we become over time. Decision-making during our life's journey is inescapable as is the irony that our journey ends when decision-making stops.

In order to make quality decisions we must create and sustain a leadership zone that shapes a broad horizon of possibilities for our life's journey. This leadership zone helps us filter through and interpret the plethora of shared observations that come to us through a multitude of sources. The zone triggers us to take inventory of what we know, and how we know it, and dig deeply into the domain of what we do not know. We acknowledge and share learning from mistakes, appreciate the significance of time on our lives and in the moment, and make quality decisions for ourselves and our organizations to achieve the fullest potential.

## References

1   Rock, D., & Page, L. J. (2009). *Coaching with the brain in mind: Foundations for practice*. Hoboken, NJ: Wiley.
2   Kahneman, D., Sibony, O., & Sunstein, C. R. (2021). Good moods often lead to bad judgments. *The Wall Street Journal*. Retrieved May 25, 2021 from www.wsj.com/articles/good-moods-often-lead-to-bad-judgments-11620914661.
3   Stanton, S. J., Reeck, C., Huettel, S. A., & LaBar, K. S. (2014). Effects of induced moods on economic choices. *Judgment and Decision Making, 9*(2), 167–175.
4   George, J. M., & Dane, E. (2016). Affect, emotion, and decision making. *Organizational Behavior and Human Decision Processes, 136*, 47–55.
5   Elsbach, K. D., & Barr, P. S. (1999). The effects of mood on individuals' use of structured decision protocols. *Organization Science, 10*(2), 181–198. Retrieved from http://search.proquest.com.ezproxy.lib.uh.edu/scholarly-journals/effects-mood-on-individuals-use-structured/docview/213828079/se-2?accountid=7107.
6   Nesse, R. (2019) *Good reasons for bad feelings*. New York, NY: Penguin.
7   Geddes, D., Callister, R., & Gibson, D. (2020). The message in the madness: Functions of workplace anger in organizational life. *Academy of Management Perspectives, 34*, 1, 28-47.
8   Mauss, I., & Gross, J. (2004). Emotion suppression and cardiovascular disease. In I. Nyklicek, L. Temoshok & A. Vingerhoets (Eds.), *Emotional expression and health* (pp. 61-81). NY: Brunner-Routledge.
9   Perlow, L., & Williams, S. (2003). Is silence killing your company? *Harvard Business Review, 81*, 5, 52–58.
10  Schwarzmüller, T., Brosi, P., & Welpe, I. M. (2018). Sparking anger and anxiety: Why intense leader anger displays trigger both more deviance and higher work effort in followers. *Journal of Business and Psychology, 33*(6), 761–777.
11  Baumeister, R. F., Stillwell, A. M., & Heatherton, T. F. (1994). Guilt: An interpersonal approach. *Psychological Bulletin, 115*(2), 243–267.
12  Lindebaum, D., Jordan, P. J., & Morris, L. (2016). Symmetrical and asymmetrical outcomes of leader anger expression: A qualitative study of army personnel. *Human Relations, 69*(2), 277–300.
13  Gibson, D., & Callister, R. (2010). Anger in organizations: Review and critique. *Journal of Management, 36*, 66–93.
14  Fosslien, L., & West Duffy, M. (2019). *No hard feelings*. New York, NY: Penguin.

15  Callister, R., Geddes, D., & Gibson, D. (2017). When is anger helpful or hurtful? Status and role impact on anger expression and outcomes. *Negotiation and Conflict Management Research, 10*, 69–87.

16  Scharmer, C. O. (2009). *Theory U: Learning from the future as it emerges*. San Francisco, CA: Berrett-Koehler Publishers.

17  Festinger, L. (1957). *A theory of cognitive dissonance*. Stanford, CA: Stanford University Press.

18  Yahoo! News (2020, April 21). Retrieved May 4, 2020 from https://news.yahoo. com/texas-lt-gov-dan-patrick-202838148.html.

19  *The Wall Street Journal* (2020, April 24). The bearer of good Coronavirus news. Retrieved April 26, 2020 from www.wsj.com/articles/the-bearer-of-good-corona virus-news-11587746176?shareToken=stb692366f69944fc09c27c8a37cea48f2& reflink=share_mobilewebshare.

20  *The Wall Street Journal* (2018, August 31). The world isn't as bad as your wired brain tells you. Retrieved April 27, 2020 from www.wsj.com/articles/ the-world-isnt-as-bad-as-your-wired-brain-tells-you-1535713201?mod=mhp.

21  Bigley, I. (2018). Extremity bias in user-generated content creation and consumption in social media. Retrieved April 27, 2020 from www.tandfonline.com/doi/ abs/10.1080/15252019.2018.1491813.

22  Duke, A. (2018). *Thinking in bets*. New York, NY: Penguin.

23  Syed, M. (2015). *Black box thinking*. New York, NY: Penguin.

24  Scott, S. (2004). *Fierce conversations: Achieving success at work and in life, one conversation at a time*. New York, NY: Berkley Publishing Group.

25  *Forbes* (2015, May 27). Forbes announces inaugural list of America's 50 richest self-made women. Retrieved May 5, 2020 from www.forbes.com/sites/ forbespr/2015/05/27/forbes-announces-inaugural-list-of-americas-50-richest-self-made-women/?sh=c09e3cd24c19.

26  Carreyrou, J. (2018). *Bad blood*. New York, NY: Penguin.

27  U.S. Securities and Exchange Commission (2018). Theranos, CEO Holmes, and former president Balwani charged with massive fraud. Retrieved May 5, 2020 from www.sec.gov/news/press-release/2018-41.

28  Hartmans, A. & Leskin, P. (2020). The rise and fall of Elizabeth Holmes, who started Theranos when she was 19 and became the world's youngest female billionaire but will now face a trial over "massive fraud" in July 2020. *Business Insider*. Retrieved May 4, 2020 from www.businessinsider.com/ theranos-founder-ceo-elizabeth-holmes-life-story-bio-2018-4?r=US&IR=T.

29  Millman, D. (2000). *The way of the peaceful warrior*. Tiburon, CA: New World Library.

30  Schorr, R., & Salva, V. (2007). *Peaceful Warrior*. United States: Lionsgate.

31  *The Guardian* (2020, March 13). Retrieved May 6, 2020 from www.theguardian. com/world/2020/mar/13/first-covid-19-case-happened-in-november-china-government-records-show-report.

32  Hudson Institute (2020). Coronavirus Timeline. Retrieved May 6, 2020 from www.hudson.org/research/15920-coronavirus-timeline.

33  Center on Education and the Workforce. (n.d.). *Tracking COVID-19 unemployment and job losses*. Georgetown University. Retrieved May 6, 2020 from https://cew. georgetown.edu/cew-reports/jobtracker/#tool-3-tracking.

34  Wheatley, M. J. (2006). *Leadership and the new science: Discovering order in a chaotic world* (3rd ed.). San Francisco, CA: Berrett-Koehler Publishers.

35  Heifetz, R., & Linsky, M. (2017) *Leadership on the line*. Boston, MA: Harvard Business Review Press.

36  Tigner, T. (2019) *Leonardo and Gabriel*. Monee, I: Self Published.

37  Eagleman, D. (2011) *Incognito: The secret lives of the brain*. New York, NY: Pantheon Books.

38  Meltwater Social Solutions (n.d.). How social media algorithms work. Retrieved May 9, 2020 https://sysomos.com/wp-content/uploads/2019/08/Social_Media_Algorithms_Ebook-1.pdf.

39  Hootsuite (2021). How does your YouTube Algorithm work in 2021? The complete guide. Retrieved May 9, 2020 from https://blog.hootsuite.com/how-the-youtube-algorithm-works/.

40  *diggit magazine* (n.d.). Is Google politically biased? Retrieved May 9, 2020 from https://www.diggitmagazine.com/articles/google-politically-biased.

41  Leonard Cohen (1992). "Anthem." *The Future*. Columbia.

42  Adams, S. (2019) *Loserthink*. New York, NY: Penguin.

43  Gilbert, D. (2006). *Stumbling on happiness*. New York, NY: Random House.

44  Orlowski, J. (2020). *The social dilemma*. United States: Netflix.

45  BP (n.d.). Retrieved November 20, 2020 from www.bp.com/en/global/corporate/who-we-are/our-ambition.html.

46  CNBC (2020, 30 June). Tesla and the science behind the next generation, lower-cost, "million-mile" electric-car battery. Retrieved November 20, 2020 from www.cnbc.com/2020/06/30/tesla-and-the-science-of-low-cost-next-gen-ev-million-mile-battery.html.

47  *The Wall Street Journal* (2020, August 6). Lisa Su's AMD is flying high as rival chip maker Intel stumbles. Retrieved November 20, 2020 from www.wsj.com/articles/lisa-sus-amd-is-flying-high-as-rival-chip-maker-intel-stumbles-11596732408?mod=article_inline.

48  Cooper, J. (2019). Cognitive dissonance: Where we've been and where we're going. *International Review of Social Psychology*, *32*(1), 7, 1–11.

49  Elliot, A., & Devine, P. (1994). On the motivational nature of cognitive dissonance: Dissonance as psychological discomfort. *Journal of Personality and Social Psychology*, *67*, 382–394.

50  Croyle, R. T., & Cooper, J. (1983). Dissonance arousal: Physiological evidence. *Journal of Personality and Social Psychology*, *45*, 782–791.

51  Copley Raff (2017, June 25). When leadership is fraught with cognitive dissonance. Retrieved December 15, 2020 from www.copleyraff.com/2017/06/25/when-leadership-is-fraught-with-cognitive-dissonance/.

52  Adams, J. S. (1961). Reduction of cognitive dissonance by seeking consonant information. *The Journal of Abnormal and Social Psychology*, *62*(1), 74–78.

53  Jim Tamm (n.d.). First steps to collaboration? Don't be so defensive. TED. Retrieved December 15, 2020 from www.ted.com/talks/jim_tamm_first_step_to_collaboration_don_t_be_so_defensive#t-766008.

54  Turvey, B., & Freeman, J. (2012). Jury psychology, *Encyclopedia of Human Behavior* (2nd ed.), 495–502.

# 4 IT'S ALL ABOUT THE GLOW

Years ago, when I, Al, was a junior executive on the rise, I attended my first executive management conference. There were a bunch of us young newbies mixed in amongst the older executives. During a break-out session, the CFO of the company was assigned the task of coordinating our small workgroup. He literally was a "gray beard," having a massive bush under his nose that covered his lips, chin, and most of his face. When he spoke, which was not often, you could not see his mouth move through his beard. It was weird. We knew he had a mouth because a smoking pipe was hanging out of it. In one pensive moment during a discussion about employee development, he uttered, "You can tell when the young managers lose it, you know, the drive to achieve. You can see it in their eyes – they lose the glow." He was staring directly at me when he said it. We younger folks shared curious glances at each other. Bravely, I asked, "Why does that happen?" He took a long puff on the pipe, and said rather professorially, "Now, that is the question to be answered."

At the time I wondered who he was talking to. Was it me? All of us? Or, was he reflecting on some moment in his own life? The experience stayed with me for years. Morning after morning, I would look into the mirror to check on the glow from my eyes. I never lost it, i.e., "the glow," even the morning after the new CEO pushed me out the door in my early fifties.

You see, I always felt like I was going somewhere. When one door closed, another one opened, often unexpectedly. I believe what kept the glow alive was the fact that I always had someone to talk to; someone who seemed interested in me. That is, I was always involved in a conversation with someone about possibilities. Initially, it was with my dad. During my early career, it was with a direct boss, then the boss's boss; and then later it was with the CEO. It weakened towards the end of my career as my relationships narrowed. In hindsight, and ironically, had the conversations been more robust later in my career, the relationships would have never narrowed, and my career accomplishments would have been even greater.

## CONVERSATIONS NURTURE THE GLOW

We are born with the gift of language, but conversation is a learned skill. And, the big learning is that key conversations grow into the important relationships in our lives – the conversations come first, not the relationships. As it works out, our life is a set of relationships that expands along our life's journey

DOI: 10.4324/9781003036791-4

towards an unknown future. What we become is co-created by participating in relationships. Opportunities seem to occur randomly, and the causal factor is the conversations we encounter that create the relationships we choose in our lives. Box 4.1 offers some insightful questions.

---

## Box 4.1: Questions

Think about these questions:

1. What are the three most meaningful relationships in your life?
2. What did you give or receive in these relationships that made some better than others?
3. Who do you talk to about possibilities?
4. What types of conversations have contributed to your most meaningful relationships?

Given the answers to the questions, what actions should you take to increase your "glow"?

---

It is tragic when an employee's potential fades as their "glow" extinguishes. Organizations can be cruel. A negative workplace dynamic can gut the self-esteem of employees and make them feel devalued and isolated. A person can become "judged" by those in control and never given another chance to learn. What that person loses is the conversation about possibilities. Their motivation becomes derailed and their disposition towards work shifts – they stop trying. If the loss of motivation is in part due to chronic stress, the adrenal glands will produce excessive amounts of cortisol that will diminish brain functioning, impair memory formation, decision-making, and self-control. The downward spiral accelerates when everyone around them sees them as someone with a "bad attitude." Sadly, they can coast for years until the organization cuts them loose. Ultimately, their defeat is self-inflicted by their deteriorating attitude.

### Sidebar about Destressifying

When I had my annual physical a few years ago, I mentioned to the doctor that my lower legs hurt when I lay down in bed. He looked me over and instead of offering a new pill to take, he told me to read a meditation book, *destressifying*, by davidji.[1] I said, "Sounds like a good idea," and promptly forgot it after I left his office. Then, two months later, while visiting a former co-worker in Scotland, she handed me the same book and said that it changed her life. It felt like a divine intervention was occurring, so I read the book.

The book is divided into two unequal halves. The first 40 pages provide a clinical description of what causes stress and how the brain deals with it. The remainder and bulk of the book explains how each of us has the capacity to manage stress through various techniques.

In *Becoming a Leader*, we talk about how stress can cannibalize the capacity of an organization, and why it is critical to set priorities for people and help them with pacing of activities. davidji makes an important distinction between good stress ("eustress") and bad stress ("distress").[1] If something stresses us (a "stressor") and we believe the situation is positive (like delivering a career-making presentation) and we believe it is a worthy endeavor that will benefit us, then that stress is actually good for us. Eustress grows our hippocampus – the part of the brain responsible for creating memories – and it leads to faster learning, better retention, and expanded awareness. If the stressor is for a short duration, we move into our optimal performance "zone" or "flow."

However, if the stressor is extended for a long period of time, or we perceive it to be negative, regardless of duration, then we succumb to anxiety and our performance wanes. Left unabated, this stress drives a "fight-or-flight" response with excessive secretion of cortisol, adrenalin, and glucagon. Long term, such stress impairs the prefrontal cortex, clouds memory, and leads to poor goal achievement, harsh attitudes, lack of clarity, an overwhelmed state, and illnesses such as hypertension and diabetes. All of us have seen good people at work get misaligned for one reason or another and start to exhibit destructive behaviors where they become their own worst enemy, eventually committing career suicide. We often wonder, "Why don't they see what they're doing to themselves?," but that lack of self-awareness can be a manifestation of prolonged "distress."

Distress can also occur in background conversations that cause us to "awfulize" or become mentally "hijacked."[2] davidji explains why the amygdala becomes activated in such situations and shuts down the medial prefrontal cortex, leaving us with reactions based on unfiltered emotion. Interestingly, he describes how the presence of estrogen can relax emotional triggers, while testosterone intensifies them. It is all about how these two hormones impact the neurological uptake of oxytocin, the "feel-good" neurotransmitter. As he states, "love conquers stress" but he is really talking about people feeling included. A colleague, Patty Beach, uses an acronym, SHUVA, to describe an inclusive environment where people feel *seen, heard, understood, valued, and appreciated*.[3] She believes that SHUVA actually supersedes love. I once heard her say, "How can I feel love if I don't feel that you see, hear, understand, value, or appreciate me?"

Telling employees that they have a bad attitude does nothing but heighten "distress" and lowers self-worth. Alternatively, enriching their jobs with new learning opportunities creates a state of "eustress" where they learn more and demonstrate the confidence, determination, and commitment to challenge themselves to achieve their fullest potential.

## Creating Support

In *Becoming a Leader*, we described a leadership competency called "Support." It is the enabler of Patty's SHUVA and davidji's eustress. We also noted in

Chapter 2 that "providing support" occurs prominently in all three religions that we studied – Christianity, Islam, and Judaism. We believe that leaders create Support in an organization one conversation at a time by being engaged in listening–speaking exchanges with employees about possibilities. Journalist and long-time advocate for working mothers, Sue Shellenbarger, described what we call "Support" in an article titled *Why Perks No Longer Cut It for Workers*. She states, "leaders foster a workplace culture where employees feel a sense of belonging, like their jobs, and trust their managers to help them move on to a better one." [4] She reports some noteworthy research findings:

- Companies that rank in the top 10 percent in creating Support posted profit gains of 26 percent through the 2008 recession, compared with a 14 percent decline for other companies in similar industries.
- These same companies' annual profits in 2014–15 grew four times as fast from the 2011–13 period as did those of other companies.
- Exemplars of Support like Mastercard, Intuit, and WD-40 have achieved high levels of employee retention, employee development, and promotion.

We like to say, "A company will achieve its highest future potential when the employees feel that they will do the same."

Given the importance of Support in an organization, and its relevance for today's workforce, we put together the following guides for managers and employees.

## MANAGER'S GUIDE FOR CREATING SUPPORT

Learning must be inclusive in an organization rather than designed for a few "usual suspects." In *Becoming a Leader* we describe how each job should have an embedded development loop where learning leads to improvement and further learning – there should be no dead-end jobs. Career paths will vary depending on interests and not everyone will be mapped to more responsibility or a promotion. But every employee must be engaged in an ongoing conversation with someone in the organization, preferably their manager, about learning and performance. The conversations should be fluid and occur frequently rather than tied to an annual process. These conversations will be the seed corn for a relationship where employees feel valued and that people in the company care about them. The relationship should be seen as boundless in terms of the potential it can create for the employee. The fact is that no one is sufficiently smart or clairvoyant to have a lock on what another person can become. Managers should be trained on how to have effective conversations with employees. We developed extensively in *Becoming a Leader* a model for these supportive conversations which we illustrate by the *Relationship Support Matrix* shown in Figure 4.1. Box 4.2 is a summary of the key terminology.

The ingredients for supportive relationships include the style of listening and the pattern of the conversations. For example, empathic listening generates greater Support because the listener is attuned to the speaker's emotions,

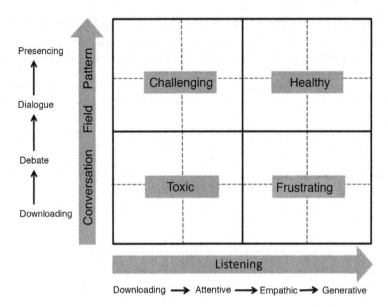

**Figure 4.1** Relationship Support Matrix

and common ground can be readily established. Generative listening creates even greater Support because the listener's awareness is open, unbiased, and conveys a sense of warmth and openheartedness. With practice, managers can learn to become masterful listeners.

The pattern of conversation is also important. Polite and cautious conversations are largely dysfunctional when it comes to creating Support. These are the "you're doing just fine" conversations. All parties must speak their minds and divergent views should be presented. These are called debates, not arguments. The manager should push the conversations even further into dialogues where all parties reflect on what is being said, thus moving from defending their positions, to seeing an emerging future. This is when the collective creativity is the highest and a true possibility might emerge for the employee.

For a *healthy* relationship to exist between a manager and employee, each party must at least be reflective in their conversations and open to each other's feelings. At the *healthiest* level, each party seeks common ground during conversations, and they listen to each other with a sense of caring and understanding.

## Box 4.2:  Relationship Support Terminology

The Relationship Support Matrix was developed by adapting research done by Otto Scharmer.[5]

## Listening Types (Described from the Perspective of a Manager)

**Downloading:** A manager confirms habitual judgments about an employee. People hear what they already know or believe. Focus is on what the messages in the conversation mean for the manager and not the employee.

**Attentive:** A manager pays attention to what differs from their own beliefs about an employee. The focus is on observations and data about the employee, known and not known.

**Empathic:** A manager sees the world through the employee's eyes. An ability to find common ground emerges. The manager can feel what the employee wants to say before they say it.

**Generative:** A manager has an open, unbiased, and caring space for the employee, and conveys a sense of warmth and openheartedness. Awareness is on themselves, the employee, and what is occurring between them for the employee and for the organization.

## Conversational Patterns (Described from the Perspective of a Manager)

**Downloading:** A manager engages with an employee from a position of what they want to hear. They are polite, cautious, and generally do not speak their minds. These conversations are largely centered in the employee's past or present situation and they simply reproduce what is known or considered acceptable.

**Debate:** A manager presents divergent views and invites the same from the employee. Both parties open up to perspectives that challenge the status quo. The manager's presumption is that there is a right answer for the employee, and they must defend their version of truth by searching for any weaknesses in the employee's position and critiquing it.

**Dialogue:** The manager shifts from winning, losing, or defending, to enquiring about the employee's views. Their presumption is that they and the employee have a piece of the right answer and collaboration is required to achieve a shared understanding. The manager and employee become reflective, willing to alter their own views, and start to see themselves as part of a system or collective.

**Presencing:** The manager shifts from enquiring to speaking into what is being created for the employee in the conversation. They speak in order to shape and nurture a possibility for the employee that "needs a voice" to keep it alive. A series of moments of co-creation occur when they and the employee collectively see a new common ground and a possibility for an emerging future.

## Support Levels (Described from the Perspective of a Manager)

**Toxic:** Managers are cautious, polite or debative, and the listening by them and the employee is confined to the reconfirming of judgments, facts, and concepts. Listening does not move past factual matters and conversations stop at debates about who knows best.

**Frustrating:** Managers are cautious, polite or debative, and the listening by either them or the employee, but not both, shifts to feelings, and a sense of caring and openheartedness; thus the frustration on the part of one or the other. Further progression to higher relationship support levels is curtailed by a conversation that rarely moves off a debate of who has the best opinion or who is right or wrong.

**Challenging:** The manager and employee are reflective and seek common ground, but the listening by both parties is confined to the reconfirming of judgments, facts, and concepts. Great dialogues and presencing conversations can occur at this level, but these typically remain fixed on business imperatives rather than the employee's development.

**Healthy:** The manager and employee listen empathically, meaning that their perception shifts from themselves, data, and facts, to what is happening with each other. This occurs through a dialogue when both parties depart from preconceived notions about each other to a more reflective mindset where each enquires about the other's views. At the highest level, the listening is generative in that multiple possibilities are perceived, and opportunities are co-created in the conversation for the employee and the manager.

Listening styles and conversation patterns are particularly helpful for managers in their relationships with employees, but they also can affect relationships outside the company. A case in point is the merger between two regional banks, SunTrust Banks Inc. and BB&T Corp., the biggest U.S. bank merger in more than a decade. According to news reports, the $28 billion deal had its roots in the relationship between CEO's Kelly King and William Rogers.[6] The genesis of the deal was huddling that Messrs. King and Rogers would have at regular banking events to discuss how digital technology was dramatically changing their industry. These huddles evoked an idea that was not immediately apparent – that combining their banks could create the scale synergies and technological edge to compete on the national stage. It is a fascinating observation that the conversations (huddles) actually created the merger possibility.

## Pace Matters

An additional consideration in manager–employee conversations is the pace of speaking. Conversations are complicated from a neurological perspective. The same words can have different meanings for different people, and people can react to them in different ways depending on their culture and life experiences. When I, Al, lived in Scotland, for example, I was amused by the culture's varied and frequent use of the word, "bastard." With a slow pace, low frequency, and curious squint to the eyes, saying "you bastard" to another person is actually a compliment about the person's astuteness or shrewdness. Quicken the pace, and with a full-face expression, the same two words are an insult, inferring that the person is despicable and thoroughly unlikeable.

Although words are important, messages and context are also conveyed through gestures, facial expressions, body positioning, and voice frequency, volume, and rhythm. Take a moment to think about what it takes for our brains to integrate all of that input in a way that a listener (an employee) perceives what actually is meant. It gets even more complicated when we consider that a speaker is competing for attention with the listener's inner dialogue. Actually, when we listen, the brain can't pay attention to all of the details from a speaker, as well as its inner dialogue about negative and positive meanings, so it picks which words are relevant and ignores the rest.[7] Is it any wonder that managers and employees can walk away from a conversation with entirely different conclusions?

In order for a conversation between a manager and employee to be in the healthy quadrant of the above matrix, a neural resonance must occur between their two brains, i.e., each person's brain must be able to simulate what the other person is thinking and feeling.[7] To this end, we suggest that managers learn to pace their speaking to employees into chunks of 20 seconds or less, followed by a pause, or a question like, "How is this landing?" or " Do you have any questions before I move on?" (You might want to test this by using a stopwatch to measure how much speaking can occur in 20 seconds – you will be surprised). Speaking at this pace enhances the probability that neural resonance will occur.

## Hugging Matters

Getting to a healthy level of support with an employee is not going to happen if the manager does not listen empathetically. In our training and coaching programs we often encounter clients who struggle with this level of listening. Clinical psychologist Lawrence Bookbinder created a practice called a "psychological hug" that we employ with our clients extensively.[8] In our training programs we pair-up attendees and assign one person the role of "talker" and the other the role of "listener." We ask the talker to speak for 90 seconds about a recent experience that has a special meaning or significance. The listener's job is to focus exclusively on what the talker is saying without interrupting them, and be prepared to feedback the following to the talker: (1) a summary in the listener's own words of what the talker said, and (2) a description about how the talker felt while they were expounding for 90 seconds.

The following results of the exercise are always remarkable and consistent with Bookbinder's conclusions:[8]

### *The Speaker*

This person is typically stunned about how long 90 seconds feels when they are speaking without any interruptions from listeners. Seldom do any of us get that length of time to speak without someone inserting their opinion, declaring us wrong, asking a question, or totally checking out. More profoundly, the speaker experiences affirmation, emotional support, and encouragement, even when these are not explicitly offered. They actually feel the emotions and sensations one would expect from physically being hugged. The affirmation is experienced because the listener took the time to truly hear them in a non-judgmental way and put the effort into trying to understand how the talker felt. It is also not unusual for the talker to make better sense of the experience they described, discover relief in the event the experience was stressful, and find clarity about any next steps.

## The Listener

This person learns that they can control their listening by tolerating another person's attitude, hold a state of openness, and suspend the tendency to judge. They act as if they have empathy for the person's situation even though they might have none. In this way they experience being fully present with another person. Their self-awareness increases by listening to another person whose values and views may be different than their own. But even more significantly, they learn that they can manifest empathy by intentionally managing their own behavior. In other words, even though the speaking–listening exchange was contrived, the speaker actually felt hugged and the listener felt good about the speaker.

When back in the workplace, we encourage managers (and all attendees) to practice the psychological hug by selecting a different employee each day to listen to in the practiced fashion. Through the function of neuroplasticity (explained at length in *Becoming a Leader*) the daily practice actually rewires the neural networks of the brain. Once the networks are activated through repetition of the listening behaviors, the subconscious parts of the brain will keep it active indefinitely, meaning that a manager (or anyone else) can train their brain to have greater empathy.

## Boundaries Matter Too

It is hard for an employee to drive for achievement (i.e., glow) when his or her manager has not provided clear boundaries about right and wrong. Specifically, leaving it up to each employee to interpret the manager's expectations is a surefire way to generate all of the deleterious aspects of "distress" among employees and to undermine their confidence. This is illustrated by Facebook CEO Mark Zuckerberg's proclamation that employees should not have to be confronted with discord about stressful social issues in their day-to-day work.[9] At the time of this writing, he announced that the company will impose boundaries to limit the internal debate about divisive political and social topics. These new policies will put limits on the use of the company's internal messaging platforms for such discussions.

In our work with clients we have observed that a documented and well-circulated Code of Conduct (COC) for employees is essential, regardless of the size of the organization. The content of a COC (and what it is called) will vary depending on the nature of an organization, but specific policies, guidelines, and consequences for violations should be defined for the following:

- Employee health and safety
- Respect for the environment
- Quality of products manufactured and/or services provided
- Cybercrime and computer security
- Acceptable use of internal messaging systems
- Ethical business practices
- Standards for relationships with governments and communities

- Protecting the interests of owners and/or shareholders
- Workplace equality and inclusion
- Employee behaviors covering everything from personal hygiene, bullying, sexual harassment, etc.

Moreover, the COC must be the subject of frequent manager–employee conversations, particularly targeted in the healthy quadrant of the Relationship Support Matrix. Without these conversations, the COC becomes lifeless, unused, and offers little support for an employee's glow. Illustrating the point, a client who circulated printed COC manuals to employees once remarked, "If today I put a $100 bill within the pages of the COC manual, I'm sure it would be there 20 years later."

Digging a little deeper into the last bullet, employee behaviors, the conversations about boundaries will nurture a culture of trust and psychological safety[10] within the manager–employee relationship. Specifically, we want employees to genuinely believe that:[10]

- Mistakes will be acknowledged but not held against people.
- They are encouraged to bring up problems and tough issues and there is a fair process for handling complaints of any nature.
- Their uniqueness is celebrated, valued, and utilized.
- Risk taking is allowed, supported, and managed.
- Help from the manager and team members is readily available for the asking.

Similarly, clear expectations from the manager about good and bad performance are critical.

In *Becoming a Leader*, we talk about the all-powerful need for rigorous performance management. It starts with goals – ones that employees can visualize themselves achieving. There is an enormous body of research about the positive effects of goals in organizational behavior. It is clear that employees perform better with clearly defined goals; they exhibit greater self-confidence, are happier, and suffer less stress and anxiety.[11] The objective is to keep employees in the "zone" of maximum performance – just enough challenge to focus their efforts on the task at hand, but not so much as to cause them to be overwhelmed. That fine line is the difference between eustress and distress.

For each employee, the following aspects of performance must be unquestionably understood between the employee and the manager and become integral to their ongoing conversations:

- Goals – *What is the employee expected to achieve?*
- Metrics – *How will the employee achieve it?*
- Measures – *How will achievement be measured?*
- Targets – *What is the goalpost?*
- Consequences – *What occurs for the employee when a target is met, exceeded, and unmet?*

Without these aspects in place, employees will be prone to a "fear of failure" that ultimately will cause them to under-achieve on everything. It is a bit of an irony. One would think that having goals>metrics>measures>targets>consequences would create stress from the weight of specificity, but the opposite is true. If this transparency is not in place, an employee will worry so much about messing up that they will not get on the field of play.[12] Thus, it becomes a pre-closed loop[12] – the glow is diminished before it ever gets to be bright.

## EMPLOYEE'S GUIDE FOR SECURING SUPPORT

Tomorrow morning while getting dressed for work, look into the mirror carefully. If you see a glow in your eyes, consider yourself fortunate because you are in a supportive relationship at work. Your ongoing effort should be on continuous learning and performance. It should also include broadening your conversations in the healthy quadrant of the Relationship Support Matrix with others inside and outside of your workplace. These conversations will expand your network of relationships and evoke more potential for you in your career.

If you do not see a glow in the reflection, then you should think about a different path. We suggest that you consider that you might need to change the way you show up at work, as discussed below. (This recommendation does not apply if you feel that you are a victim of workplace harassment. In that case, you should consult with the appropriate authorities inside or outside your company.)

### Put a Smile on Your Face

No one who can help you will want to engage in a conversation with someone who is despondent. When you walk through the door of the office or plant, put a smile on your face. There's a well-known guiding principle for extending courtesy to other people called the 10/5 Rule: whenever you are walking towards someone, make eye contact at 10 feet; at 5 feet acknowledge him or her with a "hello" or "good morning." Greet people with a handshake or other affirming gesture. We are serious – fake that you are happy. Manage your behavior rather than having it manage you. You will attract people who will want to share your enthusiasm, especially your manager. Tell them that you have become aware of all the gifts that you have in your life and you are grateful for these. Gratitude is a magnificent relationship catalyst. It will spark a new type of conversation with people, and eventually new levels of relationships within the company.

### Manage Your Inner Narrative

We have all experienced it; you know, the feeling that you are slipping at work. Your peers seem smarter, more clever, funnier than you, or the boss likes others more than he or she likes you. Our inner narratives become filled with negative thoughts and stress-inducing interpretations that play out like a plot in a Shakespearean tragedy (see earlier *Sidebar about destressifying*). Negative narratives create the Shakespearean problems, while positive narratives improve attentiveness, confidence, and work experience.[7]

For example, I, Leanne, can recount two different experiences with managers. The first was with a manager I had early in my career who was truly transformational, paternal, and developmental in every way. I would leap out of bed in the morning, work as hard as I possibly could to please him, and show him what good work I could do. The second was with a manager who was abusive, and unaware of her horrible behavior toward me (and others I later learned). She was hyper-critical, insensitive, and mean. She caused me so many sleepless nights, stress, and even tears because I could not figure out what I could do to please her. The thought of having to go into a meeting with her felt like entering a hungry lion's cage. She ultimately treated me so poorly I had no choice but to resign – I think she lacked the courage to simply fire me.

Our unconscious brains are programmed to constantly scan for threats in our lives. And we perceive threats from other people (e.g., peers, managers, etc.) more than threats from the natural world around us.[13] When we sense a threat, a part of the brain called the amygdala activates neurotransmitters that cause our reasoning and high-level thinking to shut down and emotions to drive our actions into either fight or flight.[11] In prehistoric times this was useful for survival but with today's social and organizational knottiness, the prospect of misreads and errors in perception is high. Self-control is critical because our subconscious brain is ahead of our consciousness, scanning for real or imagined threats five times per second, categorizing people, conversations, and situations as either threatening or friendly.[11]

It is important, therefore, to be aware of your stress level and seek help if necessary. Self-care is essential. Learn to control your threat response; and experience the joys of life now, rather than sometime in the future.[14] Slow down your inner narrative by inserting one second between each word.[7] This will force you to engage your consciousness and possibly quiet unhelpful thoughts.

Exercise, breathing, yoga, and meditation can make a big difference. You can train yourself in a broader awareness and get a new sense of perspective by learning to observe your thoughts and feelings without reacting to them. Eventually, you will start to understand your emotions more fully. That will give you control, and that is powerful. We have modified a famous quote from philosopher Horace Kallen to illustrate the point. "There are persons who shape their lives by threats, and persons who shape their lives by the joy of living. The former live dying; the later die living. Whenever I die, I intend to die living."

Psychologist Daniel Gilbert suggests that we create a sort of *psychological immune system*[15] (similar to our physical immune system) that defends our inner narrative against negativism. Such a system, "strikes a balance that allows us to feel good enough to cope with our situation but bad enough to do something about it."[15] A technique offered by psychologist Robert Leahy has six steps:[7]

1. Ask yourself if your negative thinking has ever helped you in the past. Usually the answer is no.
2. Write down your negative thoughts, and then put the sheet of paper aside. When you look at it later, the problems will not seem as large.
3. Ask yourself if the problem (threat) is real or imaginary. Is it part of the present or part of the past? Accept the past and let it go.
4. Instead of focusing on the problem, focus on an immediate goal that you can accomplish.
5. Accept that many problems are unpleasant, difficult, and unfair, and that some of them simply cannot be solved.
6. Take a break and focus on doing something enjoyable.

A colleague, Woodrie Burich, takes a similar approach. She coaches clients on how to discover resilience in their lives. She has created a "roadmap" which is summarized in Box 4.3.

---

## Box 4.3: Resilience Roadmap *by Woodrie Burich*

It often comes as a surprise to people that integrity and authenticity are the bedrock of resilience. These skills are required to withstand intense pressure. Resilience is commonly defined as the ability to "bounce back" from adverse events. Resilient people have the ability to withstand challenge and even turn towards it – so they may better understand and learn from it. They have honed their ability to accept the reality of a situation, while still maintaining a sense of connection or hope, despite the difficulty.

In the first instance, resilience requires us to answer these questions:

1. *Can we be in this challenge – with absolute integrity and intentionality?*
2. *Can we face reality with humility, compassion, and grace?*
3. *Can we take the necessary actions without fear of repercussion, without care of personal ego, and instead act on behalf of all parties?*

Within these questions lie the answers that create the space of resilience. It is also the space of personal leadership. They are tied.

When we connect deeply with ourselves and our core values – reflected in personal leadership (i.e. self-awareness, trust, tenacity, and humility) – our capacity for resilience grows. In large part, this is because self-awareness and personal leadership development can provide insights into our "Why." Fredrich Nietzsche's renowned quote illustrates the notion, "He who has a Why to live, can bear almost any How."[16] It is the "Why" that enables us to face challenge and gives us the energy to endure.

To build resilience at work, we need a strategy for connecting our personal "Why" with our personal "How." Two steps are needed for this. The first step is to reflect deeply on our personal motivations and values. This connects us to the foundation of personal leadership and our "Why." Supportive questions may include:

1. *What path and decisions have led you to where you are now?*
2. *What is success to you, and how is that measured?*

3. *What strategies have led to your successes?*
4. *What strategies still serve you, and which ones are outdated or no longer serve you?*
5. *If you were to fast forward in life 20 years from now, what would you joyfully want to be reflecting on – specifically, what actions and choices would make you proud, if you reflected on this moment and why?*

The second step is to find specific ways to change the structure of how we engage our work. We start by identifying and implementing resilience strategies and work boundaries – these guide our "How." Supportive questions may include:

1. *How do I feel physically, emotionally, and mentally at the end of my workday – exhausted, energized, or neutral?*
2. *What work boundaries have I set and is my work environment supportive of them?*
3. *What impact would carving out time for myself have on strategy development, problem solving, and conflict resolutions at work?*
4. *How can I bridge the gap between personal demands and work demands?*

Answering these questions and implementing the answers is one part of the approach behind the Resilience Roadmap©. In addition to the questions and steps above, it also includes supportive skill building such as scientifically based mindfulness practices, introspective tools, reflective dialogue, mindset reframes, and high-workload response plans.

For people to be resilient, they need creative time and space to focus on the deep inner work required for personal leadership, as well as strong tools to implement directly in the workplace. Leaders need to learn how to identify and communicate healthy work boundaries for themselves and their teams, implement self-care strategies for the office, and engage in honest and open reflections of the common realities and pressures found in corporate cultures. These are the steps needed to respond with resilience and help us maintain "The Glow."

*Woodrie Burich is owner of The Integration Group and founder of the Boundaries Before Burnout™ Coaching Program. Her mission is to empower professionals to create sustainable and thriving work lives that enable them to enjoy more, stress less, and connect with their communities in positive and meaningful ways. Further details: www.integratingwork.com.*

## Reach Out to Your Manager

If your manager does not talk to you, seek him or her out and just start talking to them about anything – the weather, sports, etc. Hug him or her, psychologically, using the technique outlined above. If boundaries are not discussed (Code of Conduct and performance management), ask for clarification. Find something that you have in common and let the conversation grow over time. In this way, you will become the initiator of the support relationship with your manager. Remember, the conversation comes first. It does not matter who starts it, just that one is there.

Use the listening style and conversation patterns noted in the Relationship Support Matrix. Ask yourself if you are being reflective when conversing with your manager, or are you reconfirming your own beliefs. You must seek out new insights and be open to views that challenge you. Think of your career as a good book – the further you or others dig into it, the more it comes together and makes sense. Ask for new assignments and volunteer for ad hoc projects. These could supply new learning and your manager might be able to supply what is missing. Ultimately, you want to be able to look beyond yourself – seeing yourself as part of a system at play at work – and not outside of it.

Give this new style three months. If the glow does not return to your eyes, then it is time to move on to a new position either within the company or outside. The base plan of action is still the same. It is just occurring in a new environment where you can double down on conversations that build relationships – initiating new potential for you and those you engage.

## FINAL WORDS

Igniting and fueling the drive to achieve, the "glow," among employees is essential for success, not only for employees but for the organization. When an employee has a bad attitude, labeling him or her as such does nothing good, while enriching their job with new learning opportunities will help them drive for achievement. Managers enable this through conversations that create healthy support where listening is generative and multiple possibilities are co-created with the employee. These conversations must be paced to achieve neural resonance, catalyzed via empathic listening, and clear about critical boundaries of right and wrong. Employees also have an accountability. They must become aware of how they show up at work, control their inner narrative, strive for resilience, and reach out to their managers to initiate the conversations that create the support.

## References

1  davidji. (2015). *destressifying*. Notting Hill Gate, London: Hay House UK.
2  Ellis, A., & Ellis, D. (2019). *Rational emotive behavior therapy*. Washington, DC: American Psychological Association.
3  Beach, P. (2020). *The art of alignment: A practical guide to inclusive leadership*. Boulder, CO: LeadershipSmarts.
4  Shellenbarger, S. (2017, December 3). Why perks no longer cut it. *Wall Street Journal*. Retrieved September 8, 2020 from www.wsj.com/articles/why-perks-no-longer-cut-it-for-workers-1543846157.
5  Scharmer, C. O. (2009). *Theory U: Learning from the future as it emerges*. San Francisco, CA: Berrett-Koehler Publishers.
6  Ensign, R. L. (2019, February 8). BB&T CEO shows power of positive thinking in $28 billion megadeal. *Wall Street Journal*. Retrieved September 10, 2020 from www.wsj.com/articles/bb-t-ceo-shows-power-of-positive-thinking-in-28-2-billion-megadeal-11549661911.
7  Newberg, A., & Waldman, M. (2012). *Words can change your brain*. New York, NY: Penguin.
8  Bookbinder, L. J. (n.d.). Empathy, listening skills & relationships. Retrieved September 10, 2020 from https://www.learninginaction.com/PDF/ELSR.pdf.
9  Horwitz, J. (2020, September 17). Facebook to curb internal debate over sensitive issues amid staff discord. *Wall Street Journal*. Retrieved September 23, 2020

from   www.wsj.com/articles/facebook-to-curb-internal-debate-over-sensitive-issues-amid-employee-discord-11600368481.

10   Edmondson, L (2016). Google Project Aristotle. Retrieved 26 January 2020 from https://rework.withgoogle.com/print/guides/5721312655835136/.

11   Rock, D., & Page, L. J. (2009). *Coaching with the brain in mind: Foundations for practice*. Hoboken, NJ: Wiley.

12   Syed, M. (2015). *Black box thinking*. New York: NY: Penguin.

13   Burkeman, O. (2012). *The antidote: Happiness for people who can't stand positive thinking*. New York, NY: Faber & Faber.

14   Cassata, C. (2019, September 3). Why you don't need a lot of time or money to make health care a priority. *Healthline*. Retrieved on September 14, 2020 from www.healthline.com/health-news/self-care-is-not-just-treating-yourself.

15   Gilbert, D. (2006). *Stumbling on happiness*. New York, NY: Random House.

16   Nietzsche, F. (1889). *Götzen-Dämmerung*. Also often quoted by Viktor Frankl; renowned psychiatrist and Holocaust survivor as well as author of *Man's Search for Meaning* (1946).

# 5 BREAKING THE 4TH WALL

Who can forget the opening scene of the 1986 movie classic, *Ferris Bueller's Day Off*? Ferris Bueller, played by Mathew Broderick, had just faked an illness so convincingly that his gullible parents insisted that he spend the day in bed rather than go to school. As his parents walked out of the room, he turned his head towards the camera and said, "They bought it."[1] By talking to the receivers, i.e., the audience, Ferris demonstrated that he was aware of being a character in a movie.

That screenwriting technique is referred to as "breaking the 4th wall" and it signifies the divide between fiction (Ferris the character) and reality (Mathew the actor). We use it metaphorically to signify when a person becomes aware of their inner narrative – the critical moment when the door opens to *becoming a leader*.

I, Al, broke the 4th wall in 2005, when I became aware of my role in an unacceptable reality. I was walking out of a board meeting as I passed by Shelly, the executive assistant who supported the board. She was standing next to the entrance to the boardroom and the color of her dress caught my eye. It was bright blue, and it occurred to me as a bit youthful for her, given her age and the decorum of this rather conservative company. I felt embarrassed for her, initially, and that turned into awkwardness as I became conscious that she had noticed my split-second attention to the dress. At that point, I knew it would be rude for me to walk by her without saying something, so I commented, "Shelly, that dress looks good on you."

The truth is that I felt the dress was inappropriate. Within a week, Shelly filed a sexual harassment complaint about me. I was shocked. At the time, I was the board chairman of the company and had known Shelly for about five years. Our relationship was professional and narrowly limited to the interaction of the management team and the board. When the HR director came to talk to me about the complaint, I remember saying somewhat dismissively, "How could merely commenting on her dress be construed as sexual harassment?" The director said, "Well, Al, it is not about how you felt, now is it? It is about how Shelly felt." A day later, I talked to Shelly and apologized, and I meant it.

DOI: 10.4324/9781003036791-5

## Box 5.1: Breaking the 4th Wall

As a leadership quality, breaking the 4th wall means the following:

1. Allow yourself to become aware of your role in a situation.
2. Accept accountability for the consequences of that role.
3. Take action to modify your behavior as needed.

You might ask, how did I break the 4th wall? Well, much like Ferris Bueller became aware of his role in a movie, I became aware of my role in sexual harassment and took action to correct it (see Box 5.1). Namely, I was the sender of a message through my words, but the harassment was experienced in the mind of the receiver, not mine. At extreme levels, it is easy to distinguish toxic behavior, e.g., yelling, verbal abuse, explicit threats, antagonism, violence, touching without permission, and sexual advances. However, there is a much broader range of behaviors that are equally toxic but more subtle and subjective; often these underpin major social issues like sexism, racism, and structural inequality.

### BREAKING THE 4TH WALL OF WORDS

To understand how seemingly innocuous comments can be perceived as toxic, we need to be aware of how people derive meaning from words. We all find comfort from words that connect with our mental models and experience alarm when they do not. As the HR director explained, coming from me as the board chairman, nearly ten levels in the company above Shelly, the words, "that dress looks good on you" felt threatening to her. If I would have said, "nice job getting us ready for the board meeting," that would not have felt threatening because it would have aligned with what she expected from a person of authority. Shelly perceived my words within the context of her mental model that was shaped by her career, the company, and her life as a woman. Think about it – her mental model (mine and yours too) actually is narrated in words, i.e., we think in words along with the occasional image. And, as noted in Chapter 4, the same words can have arbitrary meanings for different people, and people can react to them in diverse ways depending on their culture and life experiences. Meaning, even the same words can evoke different realities among people based on what's occurring in their mind. (See Box 5.2 Microaggressions.)

## Box 5.2: Microaggressions

Microaggressions are defined as the everyday, subtle, intentional – or oftentimes unintentional – interactions or behaviors that communicate some sort of bias toward historically marginalized groups. While on rare occasions microaggressions are behavioral, such as a man standing too close to a female colleague, the vast majority are communicated via language. Microaggressions take forms such as:

- Commenting on an Asian person's excellent English (assuming they would have an accent)
- Commenting on a woman's ability to do well in math or having a good sense of direction (assuming they would do poorly)
- Commenting on a Jewish person's athletic ability (assuming they would not be athletic)
- Commenting on a Black person's excellent vocabulary (assuming they would not have one)
- Asking an Asian person where they are from (assuming they are from an Asian country rather than born in America)
- Saying to a gay person "You don't look gay" (as if there is a look and it isn't a good thing).

These are just a tiny fraction of the microaggressions individuals in marginalized groups often face on a daily basis. While they may seem harmless, in fact, they are known to cause great distress for those experiencing them.

A number of studies have found that microaggressions can have a profoundly negative impact on receivers' physical and mental health. One study for example found that more racial microaggressions experienced by people of color were related to their reports of depressive symptoms and a negative view of the world.[2] LGBT individuals also reported feeling depressed and even traumatized when they experienced microaggressions.[3] One particularly salient example was the experiences of Black men in historically white colleges. A study of 661 such Black men found microaggressions were related to psychological stress responses such as irritability, anxiety, hopelessness, and fear; emotional and behavioral responses such as greater use of alcohol and drugs, isolation and poor performance; physiological responses such as high blood pressure, intestinal problems, and sleep disturbances. These are just a few of the responses these men suffered. And, interestingly, they could easily serve to perpetuate negative stereotypes of Black men.[4]

How do you prevent yourself from engaging in microaggressions?

- First, recognize that microaggressions are not automatic. You can control your unintended insensitivity. "Because microaggressions are often communicated through language, it is very important to pay attention to how we talk, especially in the workplace and other social institutions like classrooms, courtrooms, and so on," says Christine Mallinson, professor of language, literacy, and culture at the University of Maryland.[5]
- Notice what you notice. When you meet someone you typically "size them up" which includes noticing what about them is different from yourself. Stop right there and acknowledge that different isn't bad nor is it necessary to comment on it. Then, ask yourself if you are making any stereotypic assumptions and try not to go there. Lean into empathy. Try to put yourself in the other's shoes. For example, if you are in a group and all but one of you is of the white majority group, ask yourself how it would feel to be that person of color.

Moreover, Shelly's and my realities were each limited by the observations we chose at that moment. As is true for all of us, we select our observations based on our entire lifetime of accumulated experiences and beliefs. René Descartes' famous quote (1619) is illustrative, "something that I thought I was seeing with my eyes is in fact grasped solely by the faculty of judgement in my mind."[7] As explained in Chapter 3, observation is inherently biased. Unconsciously, we ignore information that does not confirm our pre-existing views (Confirmation Bias), and we reframe evidence that disagrees with our belief (Cognitive Dissonance). What we pay attention to becomes our reality. When we perceive threats, these become the lens through which we see our world, and so every interaction seems threatening, leading to feelings of distress. Imagine having dealt with an abusive supervisor. Even when that supervisor is no longer your boss you watch carefully for signs from the new supervisor that similar behavior might occur. Chapter 4 described how distress triggers hormones and neurotransmitters in the brain that impair memory functioning and decision-making. If left unchecked, this chain reaction can hijack our ability to respond effectively, and instead drive a person into a state of disequilibrium, earmarked by either flight-or-fight behavior.

As a result it is critical for leaders to "break the 4th wall" when it comes to words. The first step is to become aware that words matter to people in different ways; there are four more steps as shown in Box 5.3. We co-opted steps 2–5 from work done by Andrew Newberg and Mark Walden.[6]

## Box 5.3: Five Steps for Breaking the 4th Wall of Words

1. Become aware that words matter to people in different ways. Watch others' body language that may signal your words were perceived in an unintended way.
2. Before speaking, ask yourself if the listeners can hear what you are about to say without becoming upset.
3. If the answer is anything other than yes, "put the thought aside for a moment, or write it down on a piece of paper."[6]
4. Let time provide the opportunity for you to fashion your message differently or for the listeners to be more receptive.
5. If you blunder, or accidently engage in a microaggression, an apology is always best along with showing an interest in understanding how the listeners were affected. Also, ask what you can do differently in the future.

Here is an example of a blunder with the 4th wall of words. On June 16, 2020 Wells Fargo CEO Charlie Scharf sent a memo to employees suggesting that the lack of Black employees at the bank was due to a small talent pool. His exact words were, "While it might sound like an excuse, the unfortunate reality is that there is a very limited pool of Black talent to recruit from."[4] His words triggered anguish among Wells Fargo employees and recoil from the media, legislators, and regulators at a time that the world was struggling with reported police brutality and racial inequality. His apology was appropriate, "I apologize for making an insensitive comment reflecting my own unconscious bias … and there is no question Wells Fargo has to make meaningful progress to increase diverse representation."[12] By mentioning his unconscious bias Mr. Scharf has taken Step 1 in breaking the 4th wall – he's acknowledged that words matter to people in different ways. Clearly, had he followed Steps 2–4 initially he would have not needed to take Step 5.

In Chapter 3 we talked about a leader's need to be mindful of socialized observations. Now, we extend this mindfulness to include socialized words. We have already stressed that words can have arbitrary meanings for individual people, but these meanings can also become socialized in networks of people with common narratives. Words don't change but their meaning does as group narratives adapt to meet shifting context and ideologies. We were reminded of this during the fallout of 2017's #MeToo movement when sexist attitudes were revealed in words that are woven into everyday vocabulary like mankind, mistress, ditsy, man-made, cute, chairman, feisty, bubbly, headmaster, Debbie downer, and girl (when referring to an adult woman).[9,10] It emerged again relative to transgender sensitivity with the push by the LGBT community for gender neutral words like "pupils and "students" instead of "young women" or "young ladies."[10] And as of this writing in 2020, the Black Lives Matter movement has heightened awareness of words and phrases with racist connotations like master bedroom, black lists, black mark, whitelists, masterclass, Masters Tournament, and peanut gallery.[11]

Some commentators dismiss the concern about words as the machinations of "ideological grievance-mongers (who want) to decide which words we're allowed to use … as a way to exert power over our thoughts."[12] They look to the etymology of words as a way to "intellectualize away" the concerns about racism, sexism, and exclusion. We do not support this approach for leaders. As noted in Chapter 3, leaders do not dismiss shifts in their environments; they detect them, confront them, and adapt as a way to create opportunities for progress. To do otherwise, leads to being FUC'ed. No individual, organization, or institution is insulated from this reality.

A case in point is the Catholic Church. The teaching of the Church explicitly states that "marriage' is between a man and a woman. But in a recent documentary film, Pope Francis proposed "civil union" as a way for the Church to be inclusive and accept same-sex couples.[13] The Church is using words – civil union vs. marriage – to create distinctions that allow it to confront and adapt to shifting environments. The Pope states, "Homosexuals have a right to be part of the family. They're children of God and have a right to a family. Nobody should be thrown out or be made miserable because of it."[13]

## BREAKING THE 4TH WALL OF INEQUALITY

We have used the word "bias" extensively so far in this book. Let's check off some of the references:

- ✓ Implicit bias refers to attitudes or stereotypes that affect our understanding, actions, and decisions in an unconscious manner.
- ✓ Seeing issues at work through a lens of hierarchy and structure can create a biased perspective, as if these are a "cure all" for every problem.

✓ Be aware that you will judge people based on your biases, and force-fit them into a model of what you think is appropriate.

✓ Al and his wife struggled to form their own opinions on the cruise ship about President Trump's impeachment hearing because of the biases of the cable news stations and their anchors.

✓ The socialization of selective news reporting has an organic personification – it is like a pandemic of biases.

✓ Cognitive dissonance is the granddaddy of all biases.

✓ Social media algorithms tend to create gradual changes in a user's behavior in what can become a "cocoon" supported by the following biases: the availability bias, the extremity bias, and the confirmation bias.

✓ Psychologists describe a "self-serving bias" by which we blame our own bad outcomes on either luck or someone else and good outcomes on skillful decision-making.

✓ Generative listening by managers creates more supportive relationships with employees because the managers' awareness is open and unbiased.

✓ The Wells Fargo CEO apologized for making an insensitive comment that reflected his own unconscious bias.

It is clear that the pervasiveness of biases in our world is daunting. The question is how do leaders get beyond this? The question has broad implications for all aspects of leadership, none more critical than the leader's accountability for the development of employees. Think about it – how can managers create Support and the "Glow" as described in the previous chapter if their perceptions of individual employee potential are biased? The conversational field patterns will be biased; the listening will be biased; the pace will be biased; the psychological hugs will be biased; and the boundaries will be biased.

A classic example is a study that looked at managers' perceptions of female employees' work–family conflict and how those perceptions influenced the managers' ratings of female employees' promotability. Both male and female managers believed women had more work–family conflict than their male colleagues which resulted in lower performance ratings and lower ratings of fit and promotability. Ironically, the study found that women actually reported *less* work–family conflict than men, but the biases were holding them back.[14]

I, Leanne, had related experiences during my career:

• On one occasion, I was explicitly told that I was not being hired because I was "at the age to have babies."

• I was once asked to come back for a second follow-up job interview wearing a short skirt.

• My mother had to quit her job in a retail store when she was pregnant with my sister because it was not appropriate to be "showing" in public.

• I did not have the opportunity to take over my father's construction business because I was a woman and the "guys would hoot and holler when I showed up on the jobsite," i.e., I would receive no respect. My brother, who was an artist and completely unsuited for the job, was offered the business and lasted 18 months. Leaving that job was the best thing that ever happened to him and the art world – he was an extremely talented artist.

- I went to school and ultimately got a Ph.D. which was far better than running a construction company in the long run … but still I wanted the chance.
- As recently as the 1990s, I was working on a client's project team with three other males and I was the "workhorse" on the project. We traveled to the client's location to discuss the 4-year plan. I was not ignored in the planning meeting; I wasn't even invited to attend it.

While overall, I feel fortunate to have been treated "almost" equally to my male counterparts throughout my career, I must relate to many of my female counterparts who would likely say inequality was real during their careers.

Leaders must go to great lengths to be devoid of bias, viewing each employee as unique and seeing the potential in them. As noted in Chapter 2, even Machiavelli in 1513 expounded on how princes (leaders) build the potential of people and communities. And, you have heard this from us before, "An organization will achieve its highest future potential when the employees feel that they will do the same."

Five CEOs were recently asked this question: When will you know we've reached a place of truly equal opportunity for working people? Here are their responses:[15]

CEO 1: "We will know when we have equal representation in the CEO position."

CEO 2: "We will know when our workplaces reflect the rich diversity of our country."

CEO 3: "We know what equal opportunity looks like: equal pay, recruiting, hiring and promotion practices, and equality in education, health care, leadership and representation."

CEO 4: "I think we'll know when a couple of things come to fruition across the entire workforce: access, experience and impact."

CEO 5: "When employees feel comfortable bringing their full selves to work and feel valued for their unique experiences and contributions."

Interestingly, the first three CEOs inferred that equality is a metric for which a measure and target could be set. That has echoes of a "quota system." The last two CEOs took a different approach. They described what we would call "a state of mind and being." Let's look at these two approaches in more depth.

## Do Quotas Work?

Here's a recent newspaper headline, "Why Are There Still So Few Black CEOs?"[16] Here's another one, "Why So Few CEOs Are Women: You Can Have a Seat at the Table and Not Be a Player."[17] Both articles lead with stark statistics: Women CEO's run under six percent of top companies and Black CEO's under one percent.[16,17] The articles highlight that there has been clear progress over the years, but it has stalled for both groups, especially at the senior manager and executive levels. Once in the C-suite, Black and women executives tend to lose out in the competition for the highly desired profit-and-loss positions that provide the critical experience required for advancement to the CEO position. Instead, they often fill executive roles in human resources, marketing, administration, or legal which thwarts their advancement to the top.[16,17]

We, Al and Leanne, are products of the 1960s – entering the workforce in the early 1970s. Affirmative action was in full swing then and intended to provide equal opportunities for members of minority groups and women in education and employment. Coming out of the Civil Rights Movement, President Kennedy was the first to use the term "affirmative action" in a 1961 Executive Order that established the Council on Equal Opportunity. Affirmative action in the United States is a set of laws, policies, guidelines, and administrative practices intended to end and correct the effects of a specific form of discrimination.

Affirmative action first began to be enforced by President Johnson in 1966. In some cases, quotas were implemented but their effectiveness has been hotly debated and litigated from the very beginning. It continues now, nearly 60 years later, evidenced by recent lawsuits involving Harvard University's and Yale University's quotas on Asian American student admissions[18,19] and the State of California's actions establishing diversity quotas at the highest corporate level, the board of directors of publicly traded companies.[20]

California's new board quotas include people who identify as women, Black, African American, Hispanic, Latino, Asian, Pacific Islander, Native American, Native Hawaiian, or Alaska Native, or who identify as gay, lesbian, bisexual, or transgender.[20] The most recent bill requires all public companies headquartered in California to have at least one board member from an underrepresented community by 2021 and for companies to have a minimum of three by the end of 2022, depending on the size of the board. California is the only state as of this writing to legislate board quotas in this way.

While mandatory quotas serve to increase diversity, diversity for the sake of merely specifying gender and race of groups has a number of downsides. One problem is that quotas restrict the pool of candidates to choose from for opportunities, effectively limiting the process of talent development in organizations. For example, when Joe Biden said he was going to select a woman for his running mate in 2020, he effectively restricted the available pool of talent for the VP position.

Quotas reduce people to a category, segregating them by race, color, gender, etc., and judging their potential and development needs accordingly, rather than based on their individual behavior, character, and merit. A leader's job is to develop all employees to achieve their fullest potential, not just some categories of employees and certainly not some employees at the expense of others.

A second major problem with quotas is the individual hired as a result of a quota is often stereotyped as less competent because they were hired due to their personal characteristic(s). Research has demonstrated that when an individual is perceived to have been an "affirmative action hire" they are perceived as less competent. Additionally, the AA hire himself or herself often suffers from self-doubt, lower self-perceived competence, and negative emotions. Leaders must be extremely cautious if quotas are used to ensure that all employees understand the skills and experience that a new hire or newly promoted individual brings to the job and that they are highly qualified for the position.[21]

A third significant downside is that majority members may feel reverse discrimination. Giving one person preference over another merely due to a demographic characteristic is basically discriminating against members of a different group (the majority) who may be more qualified. This leads to feelings of resentment and marginalization from the groups of employees who fall out of the targeted zones.

Take myself, Al, as an example. My race and gender (white male) put me center stage as either a culprit or beneficiary of unjust or prejudicial treatment. Although my recognition and understanding of gender- and raced-based discrimination heightened throughout my career, I didn't feel that I was particularly blessed with advantaged treatment. Getting ahead for me was a constant battle – requiring enormous sacrifices in my personal and family life. Competition among peers for the best jobs was intense. Long working hours, difficult bosses, many setbacks, and the advancement of others who I felt less worthy than me were struggles that I dealt with constantly. In addition, I felt that my Italian American heritage was a hindrance, particularly as the popular and successful film series, *The Godfather*, was launched as I started my working career. The films portrayed my ethnicity as criminal, ignorant, and un-American. In hindsight, even as a white male, I question whether the success I achieved was worth the pressure and costs that I endured. Surely, I'm not alone with this thought among the ageing survivors of the war called "achieving career success."

Quotas achieve positive movement by putting legal limits on the *behavior of selection for opportunities*, but they have negative consequences, and they do not eliminate bias; rather they redefine it as systemic (see Box 5.4). Meaning, since the affirmative action (quotas) didn't achieve the desired outcomes over the last 60 years, the logical extension is that the problem must be systemic, i.e., the consequence of systems and structures created by people which have embedded procedures and processes to disadvantage certain groups of people and favor others.

## Box 5.4: Systemic Bias

"Systemic bias is prejudice, bigotry, or unfairness directed by health, educational, government, judicial, legal, religious, political, financial, media, or cultural institutions towards individuals of an oppressed or marginalized group."[22] It is distinguished from unconscious or implicit bias (see Chapter 1, Box 1.2) in that unconscious bias is directed by an individual toward another individual, and the directing individual is unaware of his or her bias. Systemic biases often show up in hiring or promotion practices.

An example of systemic bias is a promotion process within an organization that only considers internal candidates. If the workforce is predominately white men, for example, then the candidate pool will be the same and there is little chance that racial minorities or women will end up in the managerial ranks. More diverse hiring practices and opening positions up to those outside the organization can help reduce this cause of systemic bias. We saw this with the Wells Fargo CEO's apology above.

Using culture fit as a requirement for hiring also may be systematically eliminating certain individuals or groups. For example, if culture fit means that hiring candidates should enjoy going out for drinks on Friday after work, certain religious groups may be eliminated, some women also may be excluded if they feel this is inappropriate, or married people with young children may not *fit*. Fit may be used as an excuse for individuals to hire those most like themselves (similar to *me bias* or *implicit egotism*) which may lead to a lack of diversity, including women not feeling men fit in female-dominated organizations.

Job descriptions can also lead to systemic bias. Words associated with masculine vs. feminine archetypal strengths (explained in a later section below) might exclude women from consideration. More versatile words could eliminate the bias.[23] For example:

- *Strong* can be replaced with *sound, steady, excellent,* or *solid.*
- *Analytical* can be replaced with *systematic, thorough,* or *deductive.*
- *Drive* can be replaced with *energy, inspiration, steer,* or *deliver.*

There is a program called textio.com that will inspect job descriptions and highlight both the masculinity and femininity of words, provide a score, and suggest alternative words to use.

It is important to note that not only individuals and their behaviors can result in biases, but also organizational policies and practices can be problematic. Managers need to be aware of the possibility of systemic bias and review policies and practices on a regular basis to ensure it does not exist.

---

This line of thinking leads to the conclusion that human structures, procedures, and processes must be examined and reconfigured as a necessary step to eliminate bias. Consider, for example, how equality can be enhanced by actively seeking a diverse pool of applicants, providing family friendly work policies, and holding employees accountable for respect in the workplace. Another classic example is the "blind" interview technique used by many of the symphonies around the country. Listening to the musician without knowing his or her gender increased the percentage of women around 30 percent.[24]

Surely such examinations will diminish bias, but they dance around its root cause. An additional step is required for the perfection of equality in the workplace: address a peoples' state of mind and being and the ways these influence behavior.

## State of Mind and Being

Simply stated, we believe that leaders must adopt and practice behaviors that eliminate bias and inequality in organizations. Legislating behaviors through quotas and redefining human structures and processes are not enough to nurture true equality of opportunities in the workplace.

Harvard professor William James concluded over 130 years ago that, "The body shapes the mind which shapes the brain."[25] He argued that a person's behavior influences their attitudes, thought processes, and feelings, and not the other way around. Thus, he concluded that people could change their attitudes (biases) by altering their behavior. Neuroscientists now call this long-term potentiation which we discussed extensively in *Becoming a Leader*. Essentially, we can reprogram the subconscious parts of our brains that control attitudes and biases by using our consciousness to drive intentional behaviors.

As noted in Chapter 1, the model for deliberative behavior change is: Change = (Experience + Expectation) * Attention * Veto Power.[26] Literally, to change your behavior, and therefore your attitudes and biases, you must practice the behavior that you want in order for it to become automatic (Experience); believe that you can do it (Expectation); practice the new behavior in all aspects of your life (Attention), and stop all of the behaviors that are holding you back (Veto Power). And subtle behavioral changes can have dramatic impacts. For example, across disciplines, males tend to be referred to by title by men introducing them while women are referred to by their first names.[27] This is almost always unintentional but sends a message that women are less valued. Simply being intentional about introducing men and women in the same manner will increase equality.

Box 5.5 summarizes the eight leadership behaviors that we advocate in the NELM leadership model and illustrates how each relates to equality in the workplace.

## Box 5.5: Leadership Behaviors for Breaking the 4th Wall of Inequality

1. *Courage* to take actions and make decisions that support equality.
2. *Integrity* in standing for equality as a core value and never compromising in situational challenges and policymaking.
3. *Intolerant* of others who are not mindful of equality and calling them out when they behave inappropriately.
4. *Self-awareness* of ones' biases and the effect that they have on equality in the workplace.
5. *Self-regulation* and control of one's decisions and actions in the matter of equality.
6. *Motivation* to pursue equality with energy and persistence and relentlessly challenge its achievement in the workplace.
7. *Empathy* in understanding how inequality affects employees emotionally, treating the victimized compassionately, and appreciating that employees have different mindsets that affect their perception of inequality.
8. *Sociability* in managing relationships and building networks to establish a common ground of equality in the workplace.

Partially adapted from Goleman, D. P. (1995) *Emotional intelligence: Why it can matter more than IQ*. New York, NY: Bantam Books.

By being deliberative with these eight behaviors, leaders will shape their minds and way of being in the organization. When socialized in an organization, this discipline of behavior will focus effort and action on transforming the organization's present state towards the perfection of equality.

The socialization occurs because human beings will mirror the behaviors of other humans within their circle of influence, especially ones they admire. The mirroring can be intentional but most times it occurs subconsciously, like a reflex. Neuroscientists call this "attuned relating."[28] It is how the brains of infants develop and how they mature to become fully functioning adults (hopefully). Any parent of young children can recall the stunning (and sometimes scary) experience when their child played back to them things that they did or said. And here's an even more surprising fact: the attuned relating never stops until death. The behavior of those around us is constantly affecting the way we think in ways that are beyond our conscious perception.

Through behavioral management leaders can be on a journey to refine their character and to be role models for the organization. Along the way they will nurture others' behaviors by sharing an intense feeling of potential.

We recommend that all leaders consider how the behaviors in Box 5.5 could help reshape their organizations in the matter of inequality – and modify the descriptions to fit their context. As an example, the 40,000-member Community Association Institute's College of Community Association Lawyers has embraced this approach in an effort to eradicate racism from community homeowner associations (HOAs). They are advocating that HOA attorneys be agents of change by adopting and fostering the following behaviors:[29]

1. *Courage.* Have the courage to take actions and make decisions in the community that support equality.
2. *Integrity.* Have the integrity to stand for equality as a core value in the community and never compromise in situational challenges and policymaking.
3. *Intolerance.* Be an ally. Be intolerant of others who are not mindful of equality and call them out (gently and with tact) when they behave inappropriately. Sometimes your voice can be heard more powerfully than the victim of microaggressions and implicit bias.
4. *Self-awareness.* Be aware of your own biases and the effect that they have on equality. Take responsibility for increasing your understanding of your own privileges and prejudices.
5. *Self-regulation.* Maintain control of your decisions and actions in the matter of equality.
6. *Motivation.* Motivate to pursue equality with energy and persistence and relentlessly challenge its achievement in the community. Intentionally and deliberately engage in non-biasing activities. Educate yourself. Engage in conversations about race.
7. *Empathy.* Have empathy. Understand how inequality affects community members emotionally; treat the victimized compassionately; and

appreciate that people have unique mindsets that affect their perception of inequality.

8. *Sociability.* Manage relationships to establish a common ground of equality in the community.

## Versatility: A 9th Leadership Behavior

By the end of 2018, the #MeToo movement had surfaced at least 920 victims of alleged sexual harassment that led to the downfall of 201 prominent men.[30] Those ousted included many well-known public figures such as Harvey Weinstein, Charlie Rose, U.S. Senator Al Franken, and Matt Lauer. In early 2019, the American Psychological Association (APA) issued new guidelines that defined masculinity as a pathological state that contributes to the oppression and abuse of women.[31] The APA stated, "traditional masculinity – marked by stoicism, competitiveness, dominance and aggression – is, on the whole, harmful."[31] I, Al, a man, was horrified by what my gender had become.

A few months later, a colleague who I mentioned in an earlier chapter, Patty Beach, and her husband, Roger Toennis, spent a weekend at my lake house in Alaska. Patty is the author of *The Art of Alignment: A Practical Guide to Inclusive Leadership*[32] and Roger is a partner in Founder Advisors, an advisory firm for technology start-ups. Around an evening's campfire they explained their lifetime passion about the concept of Versatility.[33] As the last ember of the campfire lost its glow, I felt like I had been knocked on the head by the holy grail, causing some relief from my gender's horrendous state.

The word "versatility" has been co-opted by Patty and Roger to describe human systems that value and intentionally leverage masculine and feminine strengths. These strengths (also called energy) are collectively referred to as archetypes and exist independent of gender. Examples of masculine archetypes include competitiveness, assertiveness, and rationality, compared to feminine archetypes of patience, consideration, and compassion. Both men and women have masculine and feminine archetypal strengths. However, we oftentimes unconsciously value one way of being over the other. This is consistent with social role theory whose primary principle is that men and women behave differently in social situations and take different roles, due to the expectations that society puts upon them.[34]

Many business environments today reward masculine strengths and underappreciate feminine strengths, but the bias varies depending on the dominant cultural archetype in an organization. For example, a summary of 71 studies found that, compared to men, women were much more likely to be "punished" for showing masculine energy. That is, assertive behaviors like asking for a raise or talking during a meeting can carry substantial professional risk for women because it is inconsistent with their expected passive role.[35]

Even organizations with good gender diversity can end up with a dominant culture that is either too masculine or too feminine. In such organizations, this bias can inadvertently shut down (and out) employees based on their archetypal energy, regardless of their gender. Here are a few examples to illustrate the point:

- I, Al, am not a guy's guy. I am goal oriented and driven to achieve but I am not comfortable being competitive. I prefer to nurture someone than compete with them. I am extremely courageous in action and decision-making but mindful of risks – I have never been skydiving, mountain climbing, or ziplining. I play golf for enjoyment and the conversations that occur among friends, not to keep score or beat anyone else's. I would rather pound a nail through my finger than spend a Sunday afternoon watching a football game on television. I often wonder how I succeeded for 30 years in the oil & gas industry, one that had an extremely dominant masculine culture. I must have suppressed my feminine energy in order to fit into that culture. Sadly, my employers lost the benefits that my positive feminine attributes could have brought to the table, and my act of "fitting in" reinforced and perpetuated the "macho" bias that existed in the industry.
- I, Leanne, also have a combination of masculine and feminine energies. I have worked in male dominated organizations my entire career and have "fit in" while still being nurturing. But my masculine energy has not always been valued because it was out of line with expectations. On one vivid occasion a colleague who was unhappy with something I was proposing said, "You know Leanne, your only problem is that you should have been a man."
- Sharon, a coaching client has struggled with feminine energy. When we started working together, she stated, "I'm a bitch and I'm proud of it." She had suppressed all feminine energy in order (her belief) to advance in the organization. Recent 360 feedback was concerning as she learned that she was feared by her staff and her peers found her threatening and uncooperative. When her boss hired us to coach her, she said, "Can you turn her into a nice person? She needs to show some compassion and be more collegial from time to time."

The pervasiveness of our unconscious energy bias was made even more poignant during the October 2018 congressional testimony of Christine Blasey Ford and Bret Kavanaugh regarding her allegations of sexual harassment. My wife and I, Al, watched the entire eight-hour hearing. Christine testified first and after she finished, we agreed that she was believable. I commented, "He's going down." When Bret finished his testimony, we looked at each other astonished, agreeing that he also was believable. It is noteworthy that each demonstrated behaviors during their testimony that were stereotypical for his or her gender. Some journalists suggested that each had been coached extensively. She appeared frightened, fragile, emotional, and vulnerable; and she needed the support of an attorney on each side of her. He was angry, confrontational, defiant, evidentiary, self-supported, but also emotional and vulnerable. Interestingly, if their behaviors were reversed, it is likely that neither would have been seen as credible. The implicit and unconscious biases that my wife and

I (and most people who watched the testimony) have about expected behavior of women and men influenced our interpretation of what had occurred in front of us. It is frightening to think about how pervasive and potentially misleading these biases can be.

The concept of balanced masculine and feminine energy is not new. Ancient Chinese Taoist philosophy emphasizes that a balance of Yin (Feminine) and Yang (Masculine) energy is key to success and harmony. Nearly 100 years ago Swiss psychiatrist and psychoanalyst, Carl Jung, described the Anima as the feminine dimension of the male psyche, and Animus as the masculine dimension of the female psyche.[36] Jung believed that these hidden dimensions of our selves exist in our subconsciousness as sources of repressed energy. He theorized that accepting these repressed parts of our selves is a path to psychological health and wellbeing.

Given the goal of transforming the present state towards the perfection of equality in the workplace, Versatility, as a leadership behavior, is an imperative. Leaders must value feminine and masculine archetypal strengths and seek to leverage them as positive sources of power and energy. Women can be equally rational and competitive as men, and men can be equally inclusive and compassionate as women. The challenge for leaders is to ensure that men and women do not feel pressured to suppress their masculine or feminine strengths in order to conform to dominant stereotypes held in an organization. Instead, leaders must redefine cultural norms through their versatile behavior.

Author Betty-Ann Heggie asserts that wise leaders use both energies.[37] That's the essence of versatility. They are adept at both energies and choose the best course of action for each situation. For example, they know when to be decisive (masculine) in decision-making and collaborative (feminine) in setting priorities. Betty-Ann describes "energy virtues" which we have categorized into six areas of focus for leaders: Team Orientation, Need for Control, Priorities, Life Balance, Compassion, and Tenacity (see Box 5.5). We suggest leaders practice knowing when to use each energy depending on the situation at hand.

---

## Box 5.5:  Six Categories of Leadership Energy

### *Team Orientation* – Us (Feminine Energy) vs. Them (Masculine Energy)

- Us – when the situation requires collectiveness, integration, inclusiveness, consensus, and orientation to others.
- Them – when the situation requires individualism, differentiation, exclusiveness, pursuit of self-interest, and autonomy.

### *Need for Control* – Share (Feminine Energy) vs. Dominate (Masculine Energy)

- Share – when the situation requires quality listening, accommodating others, pulling people along, supporting others, and allowing others to act.

- Dominate – when the situation requires influential speaking, assertiveness, pushing people along, directing others, and establishing boundaries.

### *Priorities* – Grow (Feminine Energy) vs. Reap (Masculine Energy)

- Grow – when the situation requires collaboration, relationships, long-term focus, empowerment, and a flat organization structure.
- Reap – when the situation requires competition, delivering results, short-term focus, authoritative orders, and a hierarchical organization structure.

### *Life Balance* – How (Feminine Energy) vs. What (Masculine Energy)

- How – when the situation requires processes, practicing, problem prevention, focus on the journey, and attention to stakeholder interests.
- What – when the situation requires clear goals, outcomes, problem resolution, focus on the destination, and attention to the bottom line.

### *Compassion* – Emotional (Feminine Energy) vs. Cognitive (Masculine Energy)

- Emotional – when the situation requires intuition, expression of feelings, understanding others' feelings, and creativity.
- Cognitive – when the situation requires analysis, logic, rationality, objectivity, and reasoning.

### *Tenacity* – Patient (Feminine Energy) vs. Discontent (Masculine Energy)

- Patient – when the situation requires reflection, imagination, presence, responding, and appreciation of nuances.
- Discontent – when the situation requires action, achievement, doing, advancement, and simplification.

It is readily apparent in considering the six energy categories how the situation at hand, rather than one's gender, should guide a person's behavior. (This is what we helped Sharon – above – to understand.) It is entirely appropriate, for example, given a particular situation for a man or woman to focus their energy on "us," "dominating," "growing," "what," "emotion," and "discontent." One could imagine these energies for Mary Barra, the CEO of General Motors as she leads the company in confronting and responding to the competitive threat of a new entrant and technologically advanced company like Tesla in the electric vehicle market.

In a different situation the best energy could be on "them," "sharing," "reaping," "how," "cognition," and "patient." These energies would be appropriate for David Calhoun, CEO of Boeing, as he became head of the company in early 2020 in amidst of his predecessor's firing over safety issues, regulatory challenges, whistleblowers, employee unrest, and customer order cancellations following two fatal crashes of the 737 MAX.

The versatile leader is the one who knows which combination of energies best fits the situation, rather than being trapped or trapping others in gender stereotypes. Through demonstration of their versatility, leaders will shape the cultural norms in their organizations toward gender equality, where a full expression of masculine and feminine energy is not only tolerated but encouraged. Behavior that knowingly or unwittily demeans or discriminates against people for who they are is unacceptable in the workplace. This state of mind and being transcends gender issues and affects race, ethnicity, and all biases, effectively breaking the 4th wall of inequality, leading to a truly inclusive and equitable workplace.

## FINAL WORDS

Breaking the 4th wall of bias begins with becoming aware of yourself relative to any given situation. It extends to accepting accountability for the consequences of your presence and taking action to modify your behavior, as necessary. Leaders break the 4th wall of words by becoming aware that words matter to people in different ways. They are mindful that these diverse meanings can become embedded in shifting group narratives and ideologies. They understand the pervasive nature of biases in our world and how these drive inequality in the workplace. In breaking the 4th wall of inequality, quotas achieve positive movement, but they address symptoms rather than root causes. Truly eliminating inequality in the workplace requires a shift in state of mind and being. This is all about behavior and the eight NELM leadership behaviors will drive this shift. Ultimately, however, we believe that a ninth leadership behavior, Versatility, is required to transform the present state towards the perfection of equality in the workplace.

## References

1  Hughes, J. (Producer & Director). (1968). *Ferris Buller's Day Off*. United States: Paramount Pictures.

2  Nadal, K. L., Griffin, K. E., Wong, Y., Hamit, S., & Rasmus, M. (2014). Racial microaggressions and mental health: Counseling clients of color. *Journal of Counseling and Development, 92*(1), 57–66.

3  Nadal, K. L., Wong, Y., Issa, M-A., Meterko, V., Leon, J., & Wideman, M. (2011). Sexual orientation microaggressions: Processes and coping mechanisms for lesbian, gay, and bisexual individuals. *Journal of LGBT Issues in Counseling, 5*(1), 21–46.

4  Smith, W. A., Hung, M., & Franklin, J. D. (2011). Racial battle fatigue and the "mis"education of Black men: Racial microaggressions, societal problems, and environmental stress. *Journal of Negro Education, 80*(1), 63–82.

5  Ward, M., & Premack, R. (2021, March 1). What is a microaggression? 14 things people say are fine to say at work, but are actually racist, sexist, or offensive. *Insider*. Retrieved November 15, 2020 from www.businessinsider.com/microaggression-unconscious-bias-at-work-2018-6.

6  Newberg, A., & Waldman, M. (2012). *Words can change your brain*. New York, NY: Penguin.

7  Descartes, R. (n.d.). *Second meditation*. Genius.com. Retrieved September 23, 2020 from https://genius.com/Rene-descartes-second-meditation-annotated.

8 Shaban, H. (2020, September 23). Wells Fargo CEO apologizes after blaming shortage of Black talent for bank's lack of diversity. *The Washington Post*. Retrieved September 23, 2020 from www.washingtonpost.com/business/2020/09/23/wells-fargo-ceo-black-employees/.

9 Sexist words and terms you need to stop using in 2019 (2019). *Daily Hive*. Retrieved September 24, 2020 from https://dailyhive.com/vancouver/sexist-words-and-terms-stop-using-2019.

10 Language in use (n.d.). Retrieved September 24, 2020 from www.putlearning first.com/language/23sexism/sexist.html.

11 Andrew, S., & Kaur, H. (2020, July 7). Everyday language and phrases that have everyday connotations. CNN. Retrieved on September 24, 2020 from www.cnn.com/2020/07/06/us/racism-words-phrases-slavery-trnd/index.html.

12 Harsanyi, D. (2020, July 8). The media's war on words. *National Review*. Retrieved on September 24, 2020 from www.nationalreview.com/2020/07/the-medias-war-on-words/.

13 Affineevsky, E. (Director). (2020). *Francesco*. Italy: The Rome Film Festival.

14 Hoobler, J., Wayne, S., & Lemmon, G. (2009). Bosses' perceptions of family–work conflict and women's promotability: Glass ceiling effects. *Academy of Management Journal, 52*(5), 939–957.

15 Ma, M. (2020, September 27). What equal opportunity in the workplace means. *Wall Street Journal*. Retrieved October 5, 2020 from www.wsj.com/articles/what-equal-opportunity-in-the-workplace-means-11601136123.

16 Chen, Te-Ping (2020, September 28). Why are there still so few Black CEOs? *Wall Street Journal*. Retrieved October 5, 2020 from www.wsj.com/articles/why-are-there-still-so-few-black-ceos-11601302601.

17 Why so few CEOs are women. (n.d.). *Wall Street Journal*. Retrieved October 5, 2020 from www.wsj.com/articles/why-so-few-ceos-are-women-you-can-have-a-seat-at-the-table-and-not-be-a-player-11581003276.

18 *Guardian* Staff (2019, October 1). Harvard cleared of racial bias against Asian Americans in court decision. *The Guardian*. Retrieved October 6, 2020 from www.theguardian.com/us-news/2019/oct/01/harvard-ruling-admissions-racial-bias-asian-americans-latest.

19 Korn, M., & Gurman, S. (2020, October 8). Justice department sues Yale University over admissions practices. *Wall Street Journal*. Retrieved October 6, 2020 from www.wsj.com/articles/justice-department-sues-yale-university-over-admissions-practices-11602194974

20 Steele, A. (2020, October 1). California rolls out diversity quotas for corporate boards. *Wall Street Journal*. Retrieved October 6, 2020 from www.wsj.com/articles/california-rolls-out-diversity-quotas-for-corporate-boards-11601507471.

21 Leslie, L., Kravitz, D., & Mayer, D. (2014). The stigma of affirmative action: A stereotyping based theory and meta-analytic test of the consequences for performance. *Academy of Management Journal, 57*(4), 964–989.

22 Leesa, R. (2018, December 10). Systemic bias vs implicit bias: Why the difference matters when reviewing the report by the Ontario Human Rights Commission on racial profiling by the Toronto police services. Retrieved May 14, 2021 from https://leesareneehall.medium.com/systemic-bias-vs-implicit-bias-why-the-difference-matters-when-reviewing-the-report-by-the-e2fdd8da6574.

23 Harver.com (2020, October 24). Blind hiring: Everything you need to know. Retrieved May 14, 2021 from https://harver.com/blog/blind-hiring/#What.

24  Symphony (n.d.). Retrieved from https://gap.hks.harvard.edu/orchestrating-impartiality-impact-%E2%80%9Cblind%E2%80%9D-auditions-female-musicians.

25  Wiseman, R. (2012). *Rip it up: The radically new approach to changing your life*. London: Macmillan.

26  Rock, D., & Page, L. J. (2009). *Coaching with the brain in mind: Foundations for practice*. Hoboken, NJ: Wiley.

27  Neumann, J. (2017, June 24). Why are female doctors introduced by their first name while men are called doctor? *The Washington Post*. Retrieved October 6, 2020 from www.washingtonpost.com/national/health-science/why-are-female-doctors-introduced-by-first-name-while-men-are-called-doctor/2017/06/23/b790ddf2-4572-11e7-a196-a1bb629f64cb_story.html.

28  Zak, P. J. (2012). *The moral molecule: The source of love and prosperity*. New York, NY: Penguin Group.

29  Burton, L., Washington, W., & Hicks, N. (2021). Overcoming racism in community associations: Attorneys as agents of change. In Community Associations Institute College of Community Associations Law Seminar, 2021.

30  #MeToo brought down 201 powerful men. *New York Times*. Retrieved October 6, 2020 from www.nytimes.com/interactive/2018/10/23/us/metoo-replacements.html.

31  Komisar, E. (2019, January 16). Masculinity isn't a sickness. *Wall Street Journal*. Retrieved October 6, 202 from www.wsj.com/articles/masculinity-isnt-a-sickness-11547682809?st=9fxz5u14aspq0yh&reflink=article_email_share.

32  Beach, P. (2020). *The art of alignment: A practical guide to inclusive leadership*. Boulder, CO: LeadershipSmarts.

33  The Good Men Project. (n.d.). Retrieved October 15, 2020 from https://goodmenproject.com/author/patty-and-roger/.

34  Eagly, A. H. (1987). John M. MacEachran memorial lecture series; 1985. *Sex differences in social behavior: A social-role interpretation*. Hillsdale, NJ: Lawrence Erlbaum Associates.

35  Williams, M. J., & Tiedens, L. Z. (2016). The subtle suspension of backlash: A meta-analysis of penalties for women's implicit and explicit dominance behavior. *Psychological Bulletin, 142*(2), 165.

36  Jung, C. (1979). *Aion: Research into the phenomenology of the self*. Princeton, NY: Princeton University Press.

37  Heggie, B. (2018) *Gender physics*. Toronto, Ontario: Cremini Books.

# 6

# THAT **CULTURE** THING

We started Chapter 1 with a scene in the Broadway musical *Hamilton* when King George questioned whether the victorious revolutionaries knew how hard it is to lead. What he should have asked is, "Do you know how hard it is to build and sustain a healthy culture?" In the ensuing pages we will develop the thesis that organization culture is a consequence of leadership, i.e., a healthy culture is the ultimate manifestation of high-quality leadership. Specifically, it is a function of (1) organizational leadership, (2) the personal leadership of owners, board members, and executives, and (3) how well leadership competencies persist through all levels of an organization.

Interestingly, culture is most apparent in organizations when it is broken … take a look at what happens in these examples.

## ANECDOTE #1: WELLS FARGO

In February 2015, Wells Fargo executives celebrated the bank's increasing "happy to grumpy ratio" from its annual employee survey and offered it to investors as evidence of a healthy culture.[1] Ironically, three months later, the Los Angeles City Attorney filed a lawsuit against Wells Fargo, the most valuable bank in the U.S. ($280 billion market value), alleging that the bank pressured retail employees to commit fraudulent acts. An internal audit focused on the bank's performance metrics dating back to 1998 as the causal factor in an oppressive workplace culture.[2] According to the report, "Senior leadership brewed up a toxic mix of both carrots and sticks to realize their cross-selling (performance metrics) ambitions, slapping frontline staff with aggressive sales goals and incentivizing staff who reached their targets while firing those who didn't."[2] In the ensuing months and years many senior managers were fired or pushed out, including three succeeding CEOs. The bank paid billions of dollars in fines and the Federal Reserve barred it from growing past the $1.95 trillion in assets it had at the end of 2017.[3] Executives paid penalties and had over $200 million of bonuses clawed back. Several have been barred from service as an officer or director of a public company. The culture scandal badly tarnished the company's reputation and caused its financial performance to lag competitors, including its market value which declined 50 percent since the crisis began.

DOI: 10.4324/9781003036791-6

## ANECDOTE #2: VOLKSWAGEN

In September 2015, the U.S. Environmental Protection Agency issued a notice of violation accusing Volkswagen of installing software to circumvent emissions tests on 500,000 diesel-powered cars in the U.S.[4] The company acknowledged the deception and blamed it on a chain of mistakes dating back ten years that eventually created a "culture of tolerance" for rule breaking. As of this writing, the fall-out from the deception has grown to include the recall of nearly 11 million vehicles worldwide, multiple CEOs have been replaced, former CEO Martin Winterkorn is scheduled to face trial on charges of defrauding customers, managers were fired, and nearly $38 billion has been paid in fines, penalties, and compensation to customers.[5] The company is trying to change the workplace culture with the objectives of openness, transparency, accountability, and greater tolerance of errors.

## ANECDOTE #3: UBER

In February 2017, sexual-harassment complaints were raised by Susan Fowler, a former employee of Uber Technologies, claiming that the company failed to discipline a manager who mistreated female employees and ignored complaints of sexual harassment.[6] Focus quickly turned to the behavior of CEO and co-founder, Travis Kalanick, whose "hard-charging leadership style filters through the company and has created a culture where employees are encouraged to outmuscle one another for management approval and where the bad behavior of high performers is often overlooked."[7] Over 20 employees were fired and a string of high-level executives left the company under the shadow of a culture that was labeled as "toxic" especially for women.[8] In the continuing backlash, the company lost its license to operate in London, and eventually a group of investors forced Mr. Kalanick to resign. Uber director Arianna Huffington stated, "Creating a great culture will be key to the future success and, going forward, there can be no room at Uber for brilliant jerks and zero tolerance for anything but totally respectful behavior."[9]

## ANECDOTE #4: BOEING

In April 2018, Boeing was celebrated by the media as a company that had found its way culturally due to the leadership of two CEOs, Jim McNerney and Dennis Muilenburg.[10] Five months later, a Boeing 737 MAX plunged into the Java Sea killing all 189 on board, followed five months after by a second 737 MAX crash in Ethiopia that killed all 157 on board.[11] An investigation concluded that a "culture of concealment" and cost cutting at Boeing led to the two crashes.[12] Even the Federal Aviation Administration was blamed for "grossly insufficient oversight" and for having a "failed safety management culture."[12,13] Boeing implemented new procedures, training program upgrades, and software changes to correct flight control problems. Boeing acknowledged that employees deceived regulators to get approval for the

MAX training requirements, and that they illegally interfered with regulatory oversight by providing incomplete and inaccurate information about the flight control system.[14] Regulators around the globe grounded the aircraft for over two years, halting production, impairing profitability, and leading to the ouster of CEO Muilenburg. In 2020 alone the crisis cost the company $20 billion in addition to a $2.5 billion settlement with the U.S. Department of justice to avoid criminal prosecution.[14] When regulators approved the aircraft to return to service in November 2020, new CEO David Calhoun stated, "These events and the lessons we have learned as a result have reshaped our company and further focused our attention on our core values of safety, quality and integrity."[15]

## CULTURE MATTERS

Oppressive workplace culture, culture of tolerance, toxic culture, culture of concealment, and failed safety management culture are five descriptions of culture as the causal factor in the four business failures described above. We could have provided hundreds of similar anecdotes. Culture is often named as the culprit when things go badly for an organization. As noted in our opening paragraphs, we have concluded that culture is most apparent in organizations when it is lacking, deficient, or broken. It shines brightly as a flashing "red light," especially after the fact when things go wrong, but less so when "solid green" and things go right. When organizations are successful, we seldom hear about culture. Rather, contributing factors are named like strategy, tactics, decision-making, quality assets, core competencies, and our favorite, leadership.

In recent years, culture has received a greater profile as a competitive differentiator – even though there is a struggle to define it. According to the National Association of Corporate Directors (NACD), a healthy culture can be a "unifying force" and "support the elements of the strategy and business model in a productive way. Conversely, a dysfunctional culture has the potential to undermine the business model and create significant risk in the company."[16]

Culture is hard to see; you cannot touch it like other assets. If you listen carefully, you might hear it in an organization, and you can definitely feel it when attuned to its manifestations.

No company in recent years has been more of an inspiration for the creation and nurturing of a healthy culture than Zappos. The company is perhaps, "the gold standard for how to prioritize company culture as a success factor."[17] Over a ten-year period starting in 2000, the online shoe merchandizer grew under the leadership of CEO Tony Hsieh from almost no sales to more than $1 billion. In October 2009, Amazon purchased the company in an all-stock deal valued at $1.2 billion.[18] Based on Amazon's share price as of this writing the value of the sale is over $30 billion. Hsieh retired from the company in August 2020 and died tragically in a house fire three months later.

Hsieh's belief was that culture is a consequence of core values and "the way the core values show up in the behavior of the employees defines the strength of the culture."[19] Early in the company's formation Hiseh and fellow founders decided to invest their limited resources in three key areas:[18]

- Building a brand identity around customer service and driving it through word of mouth.
- Creating a set of core values upon which a culture would emerge.
- Hiring employees who fit the cultural expectations and training them extensively in the core values. (As noted in Chapter 5 Box 5.4 this hiring practice can lead to *systemic bias* if managed poorly.)

The overriding objective was for employees to believe in a higher purpose beyond profits and for them to see themselves as delivering a part of that purpose, i.e., more than just doing a job. To that end the following core values evolved over several years and became the foundation of the company's culture:[18]

- Deliver WOW service to customers.
- Embrace and drive change; continuously innovate in order to stay ahead of the competition.
- Build a positive team and family spirit.
- Create fun and a little weirdness by challenging employees to bring all of their talents to their job and reward them for not doing it just like everyone else, but for pushing the envelope.
- Be adventurous, creative, and open-minded.
- Pursue growth and learning.
- Build open and honest relationships with communications that lead to trust and faith.
- Do more with less by being operationally excellent.
- Be humble, passionate, and determined.

Hsieh's expectation was that the core values would become a natural part of each employee's everyday language and way of thinking.

There is no doubt that Hsieh's leadership contributed to the company's dramatic success. But core values were just a part of what drove the company's culture. There was actually a system-effect that occurred as processes and structures were put in place that not only complemented the core values but collectively enabled the culture to thrive. For example, unique training programs were designed, and hierarchy was replaced with a form of self-management called "holacracy," a flat structure where there are no permanently assigned roles and employees have the flexibility to take on various tasks and move between teams freely. Performance management and monitoring were customized to support the structure, authority delegation was increased, and each year all of the employees shared their experiences at the company in what became known as the "culture book."[18] These are just a handful of the enablers of the Zappos culture, and it sets up a deeper dive into culture as a system-effect.

## Box 6.1: Patagonia: Another Exemplar

### How Patagonia Does Things

"Success in the age of disruption isn't driven by the bottom line; it's value driven, and good leadership is at the heart of it. There is no better example than the founder of outdoor clothing manufacturer and retailer Patagonia's, Yvon Chouinard," say Scott and Alison Stratten. Mr. Chouinard was committed to saving the environment as far back as the 1970s. His first business was making reusable pitons (metal spikes used in climbing) because the ones available at the time were for one-time use only and were causing waste. His pitons became popular, and his company grew, diversifying into other gear. Today Patagonia is a worldwide clothing and gear company with merchandise sold in 16 countries. How did it go from reusable pitons to a billion-dollar company? It is all about leadership.[19]

> The lessons you can take away from Patagonia are from Chouinard's leadership. Embrace innovations that make sense, **keep your values clear, and use them to dictate practice**. Make tough choices, take environmental responsibility seriously, and lead by example – from hiring to workplace design, to setting out expectations and responsibilities. When your values align clearly with your company's activities, you are able to provide the kind of transparency that will set you apart. Success in the age of disruption isn't driven by the bottom line; it's value driven.[20]

Some exemplary lessons from Patagonia are the following:

1. **Do not just tolerate work flexibility – embrace it.**

Patagonia is renowned for the phrase "let my people go surfing" which reflects the idea that workers need the freedom to be outdoors, and use Patagonia's products, as well as the freedom to do what they love. Employees from all parts of the company are also allowed up to two months away from their regular roles to work (with pay and benefits) for any environmental group they choose. In 2020, 34 employees from 12 stores took advantage of this sabbatical program – putting in almost 10,000 volunteer hours for 43 organizations.[21]

2. **Have at least one "jaw-dropping, ridiculous" way to support your values.**

Patagonia has offered childcare since 1983. The service is subsidized, but not free. The onsite centers have bilingual programs and teachers who are trained in child development. The result? Nearly 100% of new moms return to work at Patagonia. Also:

- Patagonia pays for nursing moms to bring their baby and a nanny along on business trips.
- Work–life integration is embraced. As an example, one of Patagonia's lawyers brings his baby to his office every day. He both works and plays with his baby girl.
- Patagonia views childcare as a bedrock benefit, one that can be tweaked or expanded but never abandoned.

3. **Reinforce your culture at every opportunity.**

"Culture matters," the HR Director said. "And you know when it matters most? When you stick to it in the great times and the challenging times. You know, 2008 was not a good time for Patagonia and a lot of companies. But we did not cut health care, we did not cut onsite childcare, we didn't cut training and development."[22] In addition:

- Yvon Chouinard set out to build an "un-company" – one whose principal concern was taking care of employees, customers, and, above all else, the planet.
- Every time Patagonia leans into its values, the company seems to thrive. A quote from Yvon Chouinard: "Every time we've elected to do the right thing, it's turned out to be more profitable."
- The product innovation, the stewardship, and the happy workforce all flow out of the profoundly simple goal at Patagonia: "Do well and do good."

**4. Do not hire for fit; hire for passion.**

Patagonia uses a holistic approach to evaluating potential hires that comes from the company's unwavering commitment to its mission and values. And it is a reminder to every organization that they are hiring human beings, not skill sets or even experience. Moreover:

- "If you care about having a company where employees treat work as play and regard themselves as ultimate customers for the products they produce, then you have to be careful whom you hire, treat them right, and train them to treat other people right. Otherwise you may come to work one day and find it isn't a place you want to be anymore."[23]
- Patagonia says they read resumés from the bottom up. What are your interests, what are your hobbies, how do you spend your spare time, where do you volunteer? They hire people who are passionate about the world and love the outdoors.[24]

## THE SYSTEM EFFECT

We have written extensively about NELM in *Becoming a Leader* and we refreshed for our readers each of the Elements in Chapter 1 of this book. NELM is a unique integration of five organizational and four personal leadership Elements with a total of 43 leadership competencies. In Chapter 2, we described the pervasiveness of NELM in the works of Machiavelli and in the concept of godliness. We will now go one step further and suggest that NELM determines the culture of an organization.

At its core, culture is essentially the DNA of the organization, meaning it consists of the fundamental and distinctive characteristics or qualities that define the company. The key question is what shapes the DNA. Is it inherited? Is it created? If so, what are its building blocks? Is it prone to damage? Can it mutate or evolve over time? We provide answers below.

Our belief is that cultural DNA in an organization is a byproduct (it is not inherited), meaning that it occurs as a result of something else – and that something else is leadership. Leaders are critical, but effective leadership in an organization is beyond the individual; it reflects a system of relationships not just among people but among the nine Elements of leadership (NELM). Culture is the byproduct of these relationships.

Here is our conceptual model for culture:

*Organization Culture = f (OL \* PL) + NELM Congruence*

The interpretation of the model is as follows: an organization's culture is a function of the quality of its organizational leadership (OL) times the state of personal leadership (PL) in the organization, plus the degree of NELM congruence, where:

- *Quality of OL* means the extent to which each of the five Elements of organizational leadership is in place – or gaps exist. For example, a company might have a powerful Direction but there are no Boundaries defined for right and wrong. That is low quality OL.
- *State of PL* includes the existence of the four Elements of personal leadership along with the added dimension of the extent to which each of the Elements cascades throughout the entire organization – or blockages exist. For example, open and honest Conversations among the executive team are helpful but it is a poor state if the same quality of Conversations does not reach the front line of the organization.
- *NELM Congruence* is the degree of harmony between and among the 43 leadership competencies throughout the organization. For example, investing in quality risk management without an appropriate investment in employee welfare is an unreconcilable discordance. Another common discordance occurs when what people say or aspire to (Conversations) is different than what they do (Behaviors). This is explained further below.

The multiplicative relationship between OL and PL is significant in that each leverages off the other, meaning that organizational or personal leadership alone will not define a culture – it is how they relate to each other. Moreover, strengths and/or deficiencies in one will affect the other and ultimately the quality of the culture.

## *f*(OL \* PL)

Figure 6.1 is an illustration of the system of relationships that shapes an organization's culture (DNA). Here are some key aspects of how the system works (See Box 6.2 for an example):

- At the center of the system is Set Direction. Everything about culture flows into and out of Direction. This is where vision, mission, and values are cultivated, environments are interrogated, intuition is optimized, risks are identified and managed, and leaders shape a narrative about their aspirations for the organization.
- The vision, mission, and values guide the goals which are used to Create Key Processes, and they also are the basis for the Structure and Behaviors that enable the goals to be achieved.
- The values drive a brand identity which attracts employees and ultimately the teams (Cadre of People) that get created. Team members are

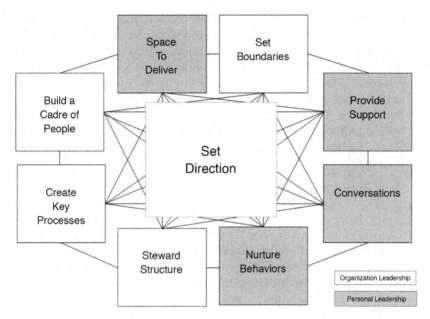

**Figure 6.1** A System of Relationships

selected based on how well they fit the desired Direction, Key Processes, Structure, and Behaviors. Members are trained accordingly, the teams are nurtured, and the potential of all members is grown while providing the teams Space to Deliver.

- The Structure creates links among authority, responsibility, and accountability within Key Processes and influences Behavior. Reward systems and performance management align with the Behaviors within an organization while nurturing an environment of Support that enhances motivation.
- The Structure and Key Processes (performance management and rewards) shape the messages that employees get about expectations. When erroneous messages are perceived it is usually due to wrong or inadequate context about Direction (vision, mission, and values). Left in a vacuum without this context from management, employees will infer one based on their life experiences that shaped their identity. Interestingly, that phenomenon is reflected in the cultural failures of all four anecdotes summarized at the beginning of this chapter. For example, Wells Fargo's aggressive sales goals without context about boundaries encouraged employees to infer values, e.g., goal achievement at any cost.
- The Behaviors that people experience when they work for or interact with the organization's management team and other representatives have a clear bearing on the system, as manifested through their decision-making, attitudes, and actions day to day.[24] Behaviors spark emotions, and

either take others up by igniting their passion, trust, and happiness (e.g., Zappos or Patagonia), or they take them down through sadness, shame, fear, and disgust (e.g., Uber). When socialized in an organization, Behaviors focus effort and action on the organization's values, and eventually can redefine its Direction – thus leading to the modification and reintegration of all nine Elements and a culture mutation.

- In Chapter 5 we summarized the nine leadership Behaviors within NELM. Although, all nine are relevant for culture, we suggest that the following have the most cultural influence (positive if present; negative if absent):

  1. *Self-awareness:* the ability to understand your moods and emotions and recognize the impact that these have on others. Self-aware people listen to others objectively and suspend judgment tied to their own values and beliefs. They are conscious of verbal and non-verbal influences and are less likely to fall victim to confirmation bias and cognitive dissonance. They are also more aware of the dangers of surrendering to the pressures to conform.

  2. *Empathy:* the ability to understand the emotional makeup of others and to treat them according to their emotional needs. It entails putting yourself in the other's shoes. When manifested as compassion it is actually a rational decision-making process that considers happiness, thriving, and suffering. Compassionate people "feel for" others but do not necessarily experience their emotions.

  3. *Integrity:* standing for something, having core values and never being ambiguous or neutral about them.

  4. *Courage:* taking action or making a decision in response to a situation. It comes from a future orientation and an ongoing assessment of the regrets of non-action.

  5. *Intolerance:* never accepting violations of the organization's Boundaries. Leaders get the lowest level of performance in an organization that they are prepared to tolerate. They signal their level of tolerance through Conversations, i.e., what they do and say, do not do and say, and the questions they do and do not ask.

  6. *Versatility:* managing archetypal energies for the situation, rather than being trapped or trapping others in gender stereotypes; and where a full expression of masculine and feminine energy is not only tolerated but encouraged. People are not lopsided by biases (explicit or implicit) that cause them to feel pressured to conform to whatever preference that they think will be tolerated. This state of mind transcends gender issues and affects race, ethnicity, and all biases that influence an inclusive and equitable workplace.

- Boundaries of right and wrong are established with particular connectivity to Behaviors through policies, guidelines, and consequences for violations. The Conversations about Boundaries affect trust and psychological safety in the organization. These Conversations shape an environment where uniqueness is celebrated, valued, and utilized; risk taking is allowed, supported, and managed; mistakes are acknowledged but not held against people; and people are encouraged to bring up problems and tough issues.

- When socialized in an organization, Conversations are tools with which people interact with others. What people talk about in an organization becomes what they believe over time about the organization, and how they experience the working environment. The physical environment of Apple in Cupertino, CA, for example, is defined by two campuses with 3.3 million square feet of space for offices, conference rooms, cafés, and health centers. However, the effective environment of Apple is defined by what the 16,000 employees in Cupertino talk about. These Conversations create the context that is socialized within the organization and contribute to its effective culture.

- Conversations Create Support through relationships (see Chapter 4) and the healthiest relationships occur through speaking–listening exchanges where all talkers are reflective and seek common ground, and all listeners focus on each other's feelings and sense of caring. A 2021 study of 24 major U.S. companies by McKinsey & Company reported that 77 percent of Black employees and 70 percent of white employees felt that they lacked Support in the workplace.[25] In these companies, Conversations are not sufficiently robust to create a viable and living network of people where the mental and emotional proximity to another person positively impacts that person's perceptions of Support and, as a result, their development potential.

## Box 6.2: System of Relationships in a Culture of Dignity and Respect

NELM influences the culture that is developed and sustained in an organization. It begins with the vision, mission and values that are part of *Setting Direction*. But the direction by itself is meaningless unless the values are clear and the other eight Elements are consistent with the direction. Let us take for example one of our clients, an Alaska Native Corporation with a healthy culture. Its core values transcend generations of village life and are deeply rooted in dignity and respect for all in the community. The corporation's *Structure* of reporting relationships and accountability are consistent with these values. Bullying and harassment are neither ignored nor tolerated. *Teams* are built with respect and inclusion in mind and leaders create a safe environment that dignifies all individuals regardless of their differences. Aptitude for, and awareness of dignity and respect are included in the employee selection criteria. *Key Processes* such as performance management and rewards are reflective of creating an environment that encourages respect, and disrespect is not tolerated (*Set Boundaries*). Considerate *Behaviors* are nurtured and modeled by leaders and encouraged among teams. Leaders work to understand their implicit biases or reliance on usual suspects in order to demonstrate respect for all. *Conversations* are open, honest, and inclusive. Performance problems are addressed respectfully with the goal of employee improvement. Leaders encourage development of all to their highest potential by *Providing Support*. And individuals are allowed to express unique differences as long as they are consistent with a value of respect and dignity (*Space to Deliver*).

Clearly, one can see that if any of the Elements violates the expectation for dignity and respect, the cultural values for this company would not be "lived."

---

In summary, it is the system of relationships among the Elements of OL and PL in an organization that shapes an invisible force that is its culture – its DNA. The system is dynamic, meaning that shifts (mutations) can occur in a culture when any Element changes. The extent of the mutation depends on the relative strengths or weaknesses of the remaining Elements. For example, the sexual harassment (bad Behavior) at Uber noted above would have had a far less toxic impact on the company's culture had the socialized Conversations in the company been characterized by robust dialogues with empathic listening (see Chapter 4). There would have been the possibility of Susan Fowler's voice being heard and embraced well before a formal complaint was filed and the CEO might have seen the need to change his own Behavior in a self-correcting manner.

Let us now turn to the last part of the culture equation, *NELM Congruence*, and explore what makes a culture healthy versus toxic.

## NELM Congruence

We have embraced the adage, "A picture is worth a thousand words" and created Figure 6.2. The figure is not easy to interpret, and some readers may find it unhelpful. We understand this but we have chosen the figure to illustrate the point that culture is difficult, and efforts to simplify it by narrowing it down to one thing or another are in fact delusional. Figure 6.2 details NELM's 43 competencies within the nine Elements. When viewing it, think of the asterisks as the vertebrae of the spine of the organization. "If any of them is out of line you've got massive pressure on the nerve and then pain all the way up and down that spinal column."[26]

Every workplace will have a culture; toxicity occurs by default. A "default culture" – one that is either not nurtured or results from a backbone leadership vacuum – suffers from spinal misalignment. A healthy culture requires effort, planning, and management just like any other strategic asset. Tony Hsieh's effort at Zappos is a perfect example. If a healthy culture were easy to achieve then all companies would have one.

(Having your copy of *Becoming a Leader* at hand as a reference for the following sections would be helpful.)

Three culture scenarios are illustrated in Figure 6.2: Healthy, Acute Toxicity, and Chronic Toxicity. Each is described below. The position of the asterisks signifies the state of congruence or harmony among the competencies (vertebrae), with *less* and *more* being degrees of discordance – either case being problematic.

| 9 Elements | 43 Competencies | Healthy | Acute Toxicity | Chronic Toxicity |
|---|---|:---:|:---:|:---:|
| Set Direction | Fracturing Ice | * | * | * |
| | Intuition | * | * | * |
| | Environment Relationships | * | * | * |
| | Managing Risks | * | * | * |
| | Managing Spin | * | * | * |
| Build a Cadre of People | Diverse Teams | * | * | * |
| | Psychological Safety | * | * | * |
| | Nurturing Esprit Teams | * | * | * |
| Create Key Processes | Accountability | * | * | * |
| | Alignment | * | * | * |
| | Assurance | * | * | * |
| | Performance Management | * | * | * |
| | Rewards | * | * | * |
| Steward Structures | Tweaks | * | * | * |
| | Restructurings | * | * | * |
| | Mechanistic | * | * | * |
| | Organic | * | * | * |
| | Matrix | * | * | * |
| Set Boundaries | License to Operate | * | * | * |
| | Employee Welfare | * | * | * |
| | Inclusion | * | * | * |
| Nurture Behaviors | Courage | * | * | * |
| | Integrity | * | * | * |
| | Intolerance | * | * | * |
| | Versatility | * | * | * |
| | Self-Awareness | * | * | * |
| | Self-Regulation | * | * | * |
| | Motivation | * | * | * |
| | Empathy | * | * | * |
| | Sociability | * | * | * |
| Conversations | Future Domain | * | * | * |
| | Proposal | * | * | * |
| | Veritas | * | * | * |
| | Performance Monitoring | * | * | * |
| | Debate | * | * | * |
| | Dialogue | * | * | * |
| | Context Setting | * | * | * |
| | Coaching | * | * | * |
| Create Support | People Relationships | * | * | * |
| | Storytelling | * | * | * |
| | Friendships | * | * | * |
| | Credibility | * | * | * |
| Space to Deliver | Step Back But Not Away | * | * | * |
| | | Less < > More | Less < > More | Less < > More |

**Figure 6.2** NELM's 43 Competencies within the Nine Elements

## *Healthy*

This scenario reflects perfect harmony among NELM's Elements and the Competencies. This is an organization with a healthy culture, as exemplified by our Alaska Native Corporation client in Box 6.2. There are no messaging gaps or inconsistencies that employees need to navigate. All of the Competencies are congruent with each other, from the way Direction is set, to the Structure employed, People in teams, Processes created, Boundaries set, Behaviors,

Conversations, Support, and Space to Deliver. The organization speaks with a common voice from the board level to the front line.

You might be thinking that it is unrealistic for an organization to achieve 100 percent congruence among all 43 competencies. You also might see this as an "ideal state" and hope that there are degrees of healthiness and some discordance among the competencies is acceptable. Sadly, that is not our experience with clients. Any level of discordance has the potential to impair an organization's culture, much like the proverb "One bad apple can spoil the bunch." The resultant state of toxicity depends on the countervailing strengths and weaknesses among the competencies, i.e., $f(OL * PL)$, as explained above for the Uber example.

### Acute Toxicity

This organization has discordant performance management and reward systems, as well as inadequate performance monitoring conversations. Employees are getting conflicting messages about goals, metrics, measures, and targets. Compensation (rewards) is even further disconnected from performance which creates the risk of poor results and unintended consequences. A toxic culture emerges because employees experience distress as they attempt to reconcile conflicting messages about expectations, and because the performance monitoring conversations are insufficient on their own to cause a corrective intervention to occur.

The messaging is critical. One of our laws of performance management described in *Becoming a Leader* is that "Employees will do whatever you incentivize them to do. They won't do anything else even when it's the right thing to do." The message that employees get about expectations is more important than any other aspect of performance management. When erroneous messages are perceived it is always about conflicting context (e.g., commenting one way about an issue in a given situation and then differently about the same issue when the situation changes), often created unwittingly by management. As noted earlier, left in a vacuum without clear context from management, employees will infer context based on their life experiences. This is what leads to unintended consequences. The Wells Fargo anecdote at the beginning of the chapter provides a clear example. Retail bankers actually committed fraudulent acts, but the executives did not direct them to do so, i.e., these acts were not intended by the executives. They were the consequence of a misplaced performance management and rewards system that lacked adequate monitoring conversations between the retail bankers and the executives.

The situation is considered acute because there are competencies in place that could limit the damage to the organization. For example, there is considerable harmony among competencies in Direction, People, Structure, Behaviors, and Support that could compensate for (and correct) the performance management issues. A good starting place would be the Behaviors of the top executives. When Mary Barra, CEO of GM, was confronted with a performance-induced cultural crisis in 2014 she said, "She could not necessarily change the culture immediately, but she could change her own behaviors. And, as she and other top executives did, there was an almost immediate shift."[27] Behavioral change (PL) ultimately leads to changes in the other Elements (OL and PL) in the system, particularly performance management and rewards which ensure that the messages are clear, and the goals are consistent with the Direction and core values.

## *Chronic Toxicity*

As distinct from Acute Toxicity, this organization is in a cultural crisis because there is discordance among most of the Elements and Competencies. The only glimmer of hope is the harmony among the Behavior Competencies. The environment relationships are inadequate, and the risk management is poor. Intuition is excessive in decision-making which leads to disconnects with reality. Despite strengths in fracturing ice and spin, the Direction set for the organization is poorly defined and the context setting Conversations are essentially non-existent. As a result, the organization struggles to attract diverse team members (who wants to work for a company that does not have clear values and purpose?), which results in like-minded people observing limited growth opportunities for the organization. Even when observed, the opportunities are rarely converted to deliverable actions because the management does not give the workforce sufficient Space to Deliver.

Management tries to nurture high performing (Esprit) teams, but the poor diversity is a constraint. Team performance is further weakened by inadequate inclusion and coaching, meaning that large portions of the workforce have poor dispositions and perceptions of limited potential. The socialized belief is that personal friendships determine who gets ahead in the organization.

All of the Processes, except rewards, are discordant with each other and the other Elements. This is exacerbated by weak context setting and excessive restructurings that have shaken the relationships among employees and resulted in a complex mechanistic–organic–matrix Structure which is inconsistent with the organization's Direction.

The poor Conversations in the organization on their own are sufficient to make the culture toxic. People are too cautious, too polite, or too argumentative, and the listening by most parties is confined to the reconfirming of their own judgments, facts, and concepts. Achieving common ground on anything is next to impossible.

The toxicity is considered chronic because of its pervasiveness. We would like to think that the strong Behaviors could be leveraged to create positive change in the culture. But it is unlikely that this would occur without some new talent brought in at the top of the company. It is possible that the entire executive team has passed its sell-by date.

The three scenarios illustrate the power of congruence among the Competencies in determining the health of a culture. Taken with the *quality* of the five Organizational Leadership (OL) Elements and *state* of the four Personal

Leadership (PL) Elements, we now have a clear picture of what determines culture in an organization.

## DESIRED CULTURE

We are going to debunk the myth that there are no direct levers for controlling or managing culture.

At this point, we have proposed that NELM determines culture, but we have discussed our conceptual model more as a diagnostic rather than a deterministic tool. (In this context, deterministic means intentionally putting in place the factors from which a desired culture results.) We encourage our readers to evaluate their organization's culture in light of our conceptual model and Figures 6.1 and 6.2. Is your organization's culture healthy or toxic? If unhealthy, what corrective actions are required? That takes us back to considering the model as a deterministic tool.

To that end, below we have provided three examples of how the conceptual model could be used to create a desired culture or significant subculture. Although the *quality* of OL and *state* of PL along with congruence among the Competencies are important for a healthy culture, particular emphasis would be required in the areas highlighted below in order to achieve each of the cultural objectives.

### Objective 1: Create a Diverse Culture

1. All five competencies in Set Direction must be in place and congruent in order to define a vision, mission, and set of values that promote equality and diversity.
2. In Building a Cadre of People employee selection techniques must be used that eliminate all levels of bias. Psychological safety needs to be established to ensure that uniqueness is celebrated, valued, and utilized. In nurturing teams, managers need to call out aggressors who might thwart the Direction intentionally or unwittingly.
3. Within Create Key Processes, it is critical to have explicit performance management goals for equality and diversity along with related metrics, measures, and targets. Employees must be aligned with the goals and take accountability for their delivery. Rewards also must be aligned with goal achievement. Hiring practices must be devoid of systemic bias.
4. Inclusion is an essential Boundary in order to ensure that all employees are in learning loops, disposed to development, and quality treatment is directed towards all employees, including emotional support, clear expectations, praise, and feedback.
5. All three Support competencies are essential and must be congruent particularly with the Processes described above. Relationships need to be tied to empathic and generative listening in order to understand what is happening with others. They must be work-related and not tied to

friendships that can be abused and manipulated. And leaders must be perceived as credible (e.g., competent, composed, and caring).
6. All nine Behaviors are important. Versatility is critical. This is discussed extensively in Chapter 5, "Breaking the 4th Wall." Essentially, leaders must manage archetypal energies rather than being trapped or trapping others in stereotypes that discourage a full expression of individual preferences in the workplace.
7. Lastly, achieving a diverse culture is heavily dependent on Conversation quality, state in the organization, and congruence. Conversational competencies in the future domain, proposal, veritas (confrontations), dialogue, and coaching are essential for success.

## Objective 2: Create a Performance-Driven Culture

1. All five competencies in Set Direction must be in place and congruent in order to define a vision, mission, and set of values that prioritize performance as an imperative in the organization.
2. In Building a Cadre of People employee selection techniques must be used that identify individuals who are motivated (and not threatened) in a performance-driven organization. Psychological safety needs to be established to ensure that risk taking is allowed, supported, and managed; mistakes are acknowledged but not held against people; and people are encouraged to bring up problems and tough issues.
3. Within Create Key Processes, performance management systems must be well developed. Goals need to cascade down from the top team to all employees and be complimented by appropriate metrics, measures, and targets. Context setting conversations will be essential to ensure that employees get the right messages about performance. Performance monitoring conversations are equally critical. Employees must be aligned with the goals and take accountability for their delivery. Rewards also must be aligned with goal achievement.
4. License to Operate is an essential Boundary in order to ensure that employees do not risk the organization's viability in the drive to achieve performance targets.
5. Among the nine Behaviors, courage, integrity, and motivation are critical, although all are needed for an ideally healthy culture.
6. Lastly, we have already mentioned performance management and context setting Conversations. Future domain, proposals, veritas, debates, and dialogues are also essential for a performance-driven culture.

## Objective 3: Creating a Safety Management Culture

1. All five competencies in Set Direction must be in place and congruent in order to define a vision, mission, and set of values that prioritize safety as an imperative in the organization.

2. In Building a Cadre of People employee selection techniques must be used that identify individuals who demonstrate safety awareness and understanding of safety concepts in the workplace. As noted before, care must be taken to avoid systemic bias in hiring practices.
3. Within Create Key Processes, it is critical to have explicit goals for safety (inputs and outputs) along with related metrics, measures, and targets. Employees must be aligned with the goals and take accountability for their delivery. Rewards (and punishments) also must be aligned with goal achievement.
4. Structure stability is needed to keep uncertainty and anxiety to manageable levels, so restructurings should be held to a minimum. Also, matrix structures for functional safety groups tend to be most effective for these professionals given the dual reporting – to line managers for performance and safety functional managers for career management and technical excellence.
5. Employee welfare is an essential Boundary in order to ensure that safety is seen in the context of all influences on the employee workplace.
6. All nine Behaviors are critical for safety in terms of state in the organization, and congruence. The research is clear: employee Behavior is the most significant determinant of safety performance. There can be no gaps between what the organization espouses about safety and the way that people behave.
7. Lastly, all Conversation competencies are essential for a safety culture. As noted in Chapter 1, there have been many studies about safety management over the years and one thing is clear – conversations about safety are critical. You cannot see complacency about safety, but you can hear it from people. You cannot see bad assumptions about safe practices, but you can hear them from people. You cannot assume that a specific safety practice is working, but you can hear if it has or has not. Bottom line: if people are not talking about safety in the workplace, then there is no safety management.

## GOVERNANCE: WHO IS RESPONSIBLE FOR CULTURE?

In the four anecdotes at the beginning of this chapter, we illustrated how unhealthy or toxic cultures severely impacted the profitability and viability of organizations. We have also noted that a healthy culture can be a significant differentiator among competitors and a unifying force in an organization. In many ways culture is comparable in value to "strategic assets," yet it is mostly invisible and exists largely as a consequence of other things – namely leadership.

As a result we believe that responsibility for culture resides at the same level as strategy, specifically, the owners of organizations or the directors who represent them for publicly traded corporations. In 2017, the National Association of Corporate Directors (NACD) came to the same conclusion, stating healthy cultures should be viewed as corporate assets ... board members need to achieve a level of discipline with respect to culture oversight that is comparable to leading practices in the oversight of risk ... culture should be the ultimate responsibility of the full board.[16]

The NACD identified a list of accountabilities for board members which we have paraphrased and modified below to be applicable to all owners and/or their board representatives:[16]

1. Get out of the ivory tower from time to time and interact with the workforce in order to get a first-hand understanding of the truths and realities held at the front end of the organization to test and ensure that these are consistent with the beliefs held at the top.
2. Interrogate, know, and manage the culture that exists among the owners and/or board members. If it is unhealthy or toxic the shadow will taint the executive team and eventually all teams in the organization. Conversely, a healthy owner/board culture will lift up an organization to achieve its highest potential.
3. Conversations about culture among owners and/or board members should occur with the same frequency and rigor as other strategic conversations. Simply stated, what gets talked about gets managed – and what we manage is what we become. Conversation is the tip of the culture sword.
4. Owners and/or board members should define "healthy culture" as a goal and drive it with the same performance management techniques as other goals, namely establishing metrics, measures, and targets, and having frequent reviews with the executive team about progress and issues. Senior executive selection and financial rewards should be tied to achievement of culture targets.

Clearly, ownership of culture at the very top of an organization is an imperative.

## FINAL WORDS

Culture matters – it is a strategic asset – the backbone of an organization. It is either a flashing "red light" or a "green light" with the former more visible when things go wrong, and unmanaged things have a way of going wrong. Culture's strategic value has received greater profile in recent years. We believe that culture is a byproduct of the system of leadership in an organization. It is a function of the quality of organizational leadership, the state of personal leadership, and the congruence of leadership competencies with the organization. Healthy cultures can be created, and toxic cultures avoided by active management at the most senior levels in an organization.

# References

1 Crowe, P. (2015, February 2). Wells Fargo tracks employees' "happy-to-grumpy ratios." Insider. Retrieved January 15, 2021 from www.businessinsider.com/wells-fargo-happy-to-grumpy-ratios-2015-2.

2 Pilcher, J. (n.d.). What created Wells Fargo's corrupt cross-selling culture? Toxic excess. The Financial Brand. Retrieved January 15, 2021 from https://thefinancial brand.com/64880/wells-fargo-cross-selling-culture-strategy/.

3 Board of Governors of the Federal Reserve System. (2018, February 2). Press release. Retrieved January 15, 2021 from www.federalreserve.gov/newsevents/pressreleases/enforcement20180202a.htm.

4 Boston, W., Varnholt, H., & Sloat, S. (2015, December 10). Volkswagen blames "chain of mistakes" for emissions scandal. Wall Street Journal. Retrieved January 15, 2021 from www.wsj.com/articles/vw-shares-up-ahead-of-emissions-findings-1449740759?cb=logged0.0073294490575790405.

5 Sun, M., & Hagel, J. (2020, September 30). Volkswagen tries to change workplace culture that fueled emissions scandal. Wall Street Journal. Retrieved January 15, 2021 from www.wsj.com/articles/volkswagen-tries-to-change-workplace-cul-ture-that-fueled-emissions-scandal-11601425486?st=52zgok4glvop6ja&ref-link=article_email_share.

6 Bensinger, G. (2017, February 20). Uber to investigate sexism, harassment claims. Wall Street Journal. Retrieved January 15, 2021 from www.wsj.com/articles/uber-investigates-sexism-harassment-claims-1487567488?mod=article_inline.

7 Bensinger, G. (2017, March 22). Embattled Uber promises change in corporate culture. Wall Street Journal. Retrieved January 15, 2021 www.wsj.com/articles/uber-will-publish-first-diversity-report-by-end-of-march-1490131194?email Token=JRryd/9+aH2SgdMyZ8wh3lAyK7YJD+vMXk7dKHHROg3CtWbO vaetxrs4ncC2vXLqX0ti4MoYqmQuADDXjC9tUoqUkqR0kRL9JygF98qdiFzX.

8 Wells, G. (2017, April 5). Arianna Huffington leads crusade to deal with Uber's scandals. Wall Street Journal. Retrieved January 15, 2021 from www.wsj.com/articles/arianna-huffington-leads-crusade-to-deal-with-ubers-scandals-1491384615?e mailToken=JRrydfh6ZHiVitUzZsw1zlwhaK8BTu+USF3WKn/WPU6JsHH crfnkzL8onNK7rCazQgN26tkAqnE+WT2UnWBnRtTUgLV2l1utf2IY982ViFbb ZhqCwQ==.

9 Bensinger, G. (2017, March 22). Embattled Uber promises change in corporate culture. Wall Street Journal. Retrieved January 15, 2021 from www.wsj.com/articles/uber-will-publish-first-diversity-report-by-end-of-march-1490131194.

10 Walker, S. (2018, April 27). One leader sent Boeing into a hurricane: Landing it was the next guy's job. Wall Street Journal. Retrieved January 15, 2021 from www.wsj.com/articles/one-leader-sent-boeing-into-a-hurricane-landing-it-was-the-next-guys-job-1524821400#:~:text=The%20Captain%20Class%20One%20Leader%20 Sent%20Boeing%20Into,a%20disrupter%20often%20hinges%20on%20who%20 comes%20next.

11 Tangel, A., & Cameron, D. (2019, April 29). Boeing chief defends 737 MAX design work. Wall Street Journal. Retrieved January 15, 2021 from www.wsj.com/articles/boeing-shareholders-reject-splitting-chairman-ceo-roles-11556551056#:~:text=Boeing%20Chief%20Defends%20737%20MAX%20 Design%20Work%20Dennis,Boeing%20CEO%20Dennis%20Muilenburg%20 in%20Chicago%20on%20Monday.

12  Rushe, D. (2020, March 6). Boeing's culture of concealment led to fatal 737 Max crashes, report finds. *The Guardian*. Retrieved January 15, 2021 from www.theguardian.com/business/2020/mar/06/boeing-culture-concealment-fatal-737-max-crashes-report.

13  Pasztor, A. (2020, December 20). Senate panel rbukes FAA in wake of 737 Max tragedies. *Wall Street Journal*. Retrieved January 16, 2021 from www.wsj.com/articles/senate-panel-rebukes-faa-in-wake-of-boeing-737-max-tragedies-11608470513.

14  Michaels, D., Tangel, A., & Pasztor, A. (2021, January 7). Boeing reaches $2.5 billion settlement of U.S. probe into 737 MAX crashes. *Wall Street Journal*. Retrieved January 15, 2021 from www.wsj.com/articles/boeing-reaches-2-5-billion-settlement-of-u-s-probe-into-737-max-crashes-11610054729.

15  Partridge, J., & Jolly, J. (2021, January 27). Boeing 737 Max cleared to fly again by EU regulator. *The Guardian*. Retrieved January 15, 2021 from www.theguardian.com%2Fbusiness%2F2020%2Fnov%2F18%2Fboeing-737-max-given-approval-to-fly-again-by-us-regulators.

16  NACD Blue Ribbon Commission (2017). *Culture as a Corporate Asset*. National Association of Corporate Directors.

17  CultureIQ. (2014, October 23). How to bring a little "wow" into your workplace culture. Blog. Retrieved January 18, 2021 from https://cultureiq.com/blog/zappos-workplace-culture-tour/.

18  Hsieh, T. (2010). *Delivering happiness: A path to profits, passion, and purpose*. New York, NY: Grand Central Publishing.

19  Patagonia: Culture & Life (n.d.). Retrieved March 23, 2021 from www.patagonia.com/culture.html.

20  Stratton, S., & Konrad, A. (2018). *Unbranding: 100 branding lessons for the age of disruption*. Hoboken, NJ: Wiley & Sons.

21  Leadership in action: Patagonia case study (n.d.). The People Space. Retrieved March 23, 2021 from www.thepeoplespace.com/practice/articles/leadership-action-patagonia-case-study.

22  Patagonia: Environmental internship program (n.d.). Retrieved March 23, 2021 from www.patagonia.com/environmental-internship-program.html.

23  Anderson, B. M. (2019, September 27). 5 ridiculous ways Patagonia has built a culture that does well and does good. LinkedIn. Retrieved March 23, 2021 from https://business.linkedin.com/talent-solutions/blog/talent-connect/2019/5-ways-patagonia-built-ridiculous-culture.

24  Protoviti (n.d.). Corporate culture: Are you curious enough? Retrieved on March 1, 2021 from www.protiviti.com/US-en/insights/bulletin-vol6-issue12.

25  McKinsey & Company (2021, February 21). Race in the workplace: The Black experience in the U.S. private sector. Retrieved on February 22, 2021 from www.mckinsey.com/featured-insights/diversity-and-inclusion/Race-in-the-workplace-The-Black-experience-in-the-US-private-sector.

26  Slot, O. (2018). *The Talent Lab*. London: Ebury Press.

27  Schmidt, A. (2020, July 12). How Mary Barra led GM through its 2014 recall scandal and changed the company's culture. FOXBusiness. Retrieved on February 5, 2021 from www.foxbusiness.com/money/mary-barra-gm-2014-recall-scandal-winning-formula.

# 7 BECOMING **DIGITALLY** MATURE

In 2001, thought leader Marc Prensky described a "singularity" that had occurred in kindergarten to college education – an event that changed everything going forward and there was no going back.[1] The event was the arrival of *Digital Natives*, students born after the early 1980s (Millennials and Gen Z's) who had been surrounded ubiquitously by "toys and tools" built with digital technologies: computers, videogames, digital music players, video cams, cell phones, etc.[11] Research has shown that more than 80 percent of this population sleeps with their cell phones, half check them in the middle of the night, and a third send over 35 text messages after having gone to bed.[2]

Prensky hypothesized that the brains of digital natives had been physically affected by digital technology because they "spoke" a digital language and thought and processed information in ways that were fundamentally different from prior generations of Gen X's, Baby Boomers, and Traditionalists. He described those latter generations as *Digital Immigrants* as they "spoke" an outdated language and were struggling to adapt to a new environment that was becoming fundamentally digital.

Spring forward 20 years to today and we now have *born-digital* enterprises, "a generation of organizations founded after 1995, whose operating models and capabilities are based on exploiting internet-era information and digital technologies as a core competency."[3] These companies grew up and are fluent in all things digital. Examples include Amazon, Google, Facebook, LinkedIn, Netflix, Lyft, and Uber. *Traditional enterprises* are those who were around before the advancements in digital technology and, much like the *Digital Immigrants* of years past, they have had to adapt in order to survive in a digital world. The process of adapting is described in Box 7.1 Digital Transformation.

This chapter is written primarily for managers and executives of *traditional enterprises* and other organizations trying to transform and/or mature in the digital world.

## Box 7.1: Digital Transformation

Digital technology has evolved over the last 60 years. However, its origins date back two centuries earlier to mathematical concepts conceived to describe words, images, and

DOI: 10.4324/9781003036791-7

concepts with digits.[4] Bell Labs is generally considered the first to use digitalization in a commercial application.[5] "Digitized" means to be stored in binary code sequences of the digits 0 and 1. Immense amounts of data and information can be compressed, stored, duplicated, and available "instantly" for use in audio and video communication networks, television broadcasts, printing, computers, smartphones, and many other applications.

A "transformation" is enabled not only by the instant availability of data but also by increasingly sophisticated computers and machines that mimic the perception, learning, problem solving, and decision-making capabilities of the human mind, i.e., artificial intelligence (AI).[6] An AI application can innovate (reprogram itself) as it digests more information, and it can teach itself to perform a task with increasingly greater accuracy, without human intervention.[6] Digital representations of real-world things, environments, markets, business processes, and people can now be created with off-the-shelf systems that were unimaginable ten years ago.[7] These digital (or "intelligent") twins "help enterprises optimize operations and predict anomalies, pivot to prevent unplanned downtime, enable greater autonomy, and dramatically adjust their designs and strategies with every piece of data they collect or new test that they run."[8]

Even in the medical field bio-digital twins are being tested for the human heart and the entire cardiovascular system. For a patient suffering from heart disease, the potential exists to predict when their condition might worsen, or which drugs would be best to prescribe. Meanwhile, online software applications (chatbots) are being perfected to either replace or aid human therapists by creating digital twins of a person's mental state.[9]

"Going paperless" is a euphemism commonly used in years past for digital transformation but there is now much more involved than converting ink-on-paper records to binary code computer files. At one level it involves companies reorganizing their *external interfaces* to meet the preferences of consumers who are increasingly connected to products and markets through a convergence of social media, mobile devices, and the internet.[10] At another level it involves a "lean transformation" i.e., changes to the *internal structures and processes* of companies and governments to drive efficiency, simplify work processes, analyze situations, and innovate in procurement, manufacturing, research, and every aspect of their operations. In addition, these changes yield data-driven insights, previously unavailable, that allow an enterprise to deliver more customized products and services. The advent of large-scale rental data centers and computing servers (the Cloud) has made advances in external interfaces and internal structures widely accessible to millions of organizations on a pay-as-you-go basis, eliminating the often-prohibitive cost of on-premises infrastructure.

At a third level, a shift occurs in the Leadership Zone (Chapter 2, Figure 2.1) of influential executives and employees, thus creating awareness of new opportunities (and constraints) that were not previously visible. When this shift occurs it can redefine an organization or an entire business, lead to new business models, and reach new customers and markets.

The roles of employees are often changed in a digital transformation which, on top of the changes in external interfaces and internal structures and processes, can shift the system of relationships within an organization (See Chapter 6, Figure 6.1) and therefore its culture. Research shows that many organizations invest in digital technologies, but equal numbers struggle to either achieve transformational effects or sustain them once achieved.[11] We believe the low success rate is due to a failure to address the nuances of our conceptual model, *Organization Culture = f(OL * PL) + NELM Congruence.*

## CREATE OPPORTUNITIES TO PROGRESS (COP'ED) OR FAILURE, UNDERPERFORMANCE, AND CRISIS (FUC'ED)

The 2020 coronavirus pandemic ravaged large portions of the global economy but it also amplified our awareness of how much digital technology has reshaped the way we shop, work, communicate, and learn. Collaboration software (e.g., Zoom and Microsoft Teams) probably caught the most attention as students of all ages and employees adapted to facility closures and social-distancing requirements. Online ordering and delivery services for grocery stores and restaurants also became prevalent, especially platforms designed for hand-held devices. But these were just hallmarks of consumer cognizance of a shifting environment. Behind the scenes, digital technologies have been impacting businesses over the last decade, propelling some (i.e., COP'ed – see Chapter 3) and making others obsolete (i.e., FUC'ed).

For many businesses the digital challenge started with how to compete with Amazon in the e-commerce world.[12] What appeared as a choice early on morphed into an imperative in recent years as digital technologies disrupted the status quo pervasively, sparing few industries and organizations. At the same time three broad trends have made organizational survival more difficult:[13]

*1. Greater Prospect of Surprises.* Organizations encounter environments today which are more diverse, dynamic, divisive, harsh, and less predictable than years back. The risk of unawareness or hidden information is heightened in such environments, and complications can emerge from unknown future information and factors.

*2. Greater Interdependency.* Environments are more transparent, interconnected globally, and interdependencies have emerged that cross industry boundaries into social and political dimensions (e.g., climate change, equality, and election regulations) which add tension and potential shocks to stability.

*3. Greater Risk of Obsolescence.* Diffusion rates of new technology (including digital) from invention to market adoption has reduced dramatically (e.g., 39 years for the telephone to three years for smartphones). As a result organizations move through product life cycles much more quickly and must adapt more rapidly to market shifts. It is a reminder about the influence of time on the leadership zone (see Chapter 3). Leaders in *traditional enterprises* must redefine their relationship with time to reflect shorter product life cycles.

As a result of these trends the need for organizations to continuously adapt to dynamic environments is compelling, and digital technology falls within this broader environmental context.

### Examples of Adapters

The top companies in digital innovation are household names. Amazon leads the pack, followed by IBM, Microsoft, and Apple in that order.[14] Interestingly, these are a mix of *born-digital* and *traditional enterprises*. Here are descriptions of a few other *traditional enterprises* that are in various stages of adapting in a digital world, some more successfully than others:

- Suncor is a Canadian integrated energy company based in Calgary, Alberta with revenue in the $40 billion range. The company contracted with Microsoft in 2019 for its digital transformation.[15] The goal was three-fold: digitally transform the retail fuel network of Petro-Canada stations, track all data collected at its oil sands projects, and change business processes at the Calgary headquarters. The company had earlier moved to fully autonomous trucks at its oil sands mines. Employees already wore digital wireless badges while in the field, allowing the company to monitor and analyze frontline maintenance work. Data from all sources was consolidated into Microsoft's three clouds (Azure Service, Dynamic 365, and Office 365) and subjected to new analytics, augmented with AI and machine learning.
- Honeywell set out in 2017 with a digital-first vision to redefine the firm's structure, culture, and brand to become more of a software company as opposed to largely an industrial company.[16] Heavy investments were made to improve infrastructure, streamline and standardize systems, and strengthen processes. A goal emerged to harness massive amounts of data, so leaders could make better-informed decisions and execute more effectively. A new business was formed, Honeywell Connected Enterprise, initially as the focal point for growing the software business, but ultimately the new business was used to restructure the four existing business units (Aerospace, Building Technologies, Safety and Productivity Solutions, and Performance Materials and Technologies) around the digital agenda. Skill sets were augmented by external hires with digital expertise and acumen. Acquisitions of digital savvy companies occurred while older industrial businesses were spun off. The transition was difficult and messy at times, and the company was ultimately seen as a standard bearer of a successful digital transformation.
- A client in the Pacific Northwest runs a multi-location retail–industrial hardware operation. The CEO refers to the company as a "tweenie" – too big to be considered a small operation but too small to be considered a major in its industry. Competitive pressures (i.e., *external interfaces* – See Box 7.1) were driving the company to consider digital investments, but these proved difficult to justify economically given the size of the operation. Industrial customers wanted to see inventory availability online before executing orders, and retail customers wanted to be able to search product availability before they came to a store to make a purchase. According to the CEO, "Customer habits have been trained by the likes of Amazon.com to view products on their iPhones, and if you can't meet that expectation, they are not going to walk in the store." Eventually, the company purchased an off-the-shelf web-based ordering system for $250,000 and spent another $50,000 to modify it to fit their needs. The

IT department led the implementation of the new system and worked closely with sales, marketing, warehousing, and accounting.

Some resistance occurred from long-time employees and there was a lot of "pushing and shoving" to get people on board with the new technology. Their website now has over a million products displayed but only 20,000 available in the stores. Online search traffic increased beyond expectations. They experimented with retail online sales and were surprised by the take up. Recently, the company invested $350,000 to build-out leased space and added 60 employees (i.e., *internal structures*) to handle replenishment and retail order shipping and fulfillment. They are confident that net revenue will grow each year and achieve 20 percent by year three. Plans include moving to the cloud in a few months, experimenting with analytics in order to monetize the enormous data being generated by the new system, and keeping a watchful eye on the next digital opportunity.

- In 2013 GE CEO, Jeff Immelt, visioned an "industrial internet" that the company would build for global use.[17] It was a bold step-out for a *traditional enterprise* known mostly for the manufacture of gas-fired turbines, jet engines, appliances, light bulbs, locomotives, and MRI machines (although the company was involved in many other industries at the time). The mission was to build "first-of-its kind"[17] software and computing capacity to harvest huge amounts of data from their installed industrial equipment and provide high quality analytics to their customers. The applications (apps) would run on a proprietary platform and cloud called Predix, which would reside in a new division called GE Digital. The company ran into trouble when the marketing of Predix got ahead of the product development. Costly investments, employee confusion, and inadequate (or poorly used) skills sets delayed app development. Sales teams were attempting to sell Predix to customers without having the confidence that the products could deliver. Also, a lot of the "big data" capabilities were already being offered by Amazon and Microsoft which were many years ahead of GE in product development. It proved difficult for GE to compete effectively. In 2017 Mr. Immelt stepped down as CEO and his successor shifted strategy, spinning-off GE Digital into a standalone entity.

## Common Pitfalls

Embedded in the stories above are some important lessons for *traditional enterprises* as they attempt to mature in the digital world. Within the literature there are many case studies about successes and failures with digital endeavors. Here are three common pitfalls:

1. *Hierarchy Myopia,* i.e., what executives at the top of the company think is happening is substantially different than what is occurring down the line where work gets done. This was a big issue for GE. "There was a lot of saluting

the Predix flag," but commitment was tenuous behind the scenes, and a "fake and bake" behavior emerged whereby app designers created animated representations of designs that gave executives the faulty impression that the apps were developed and working.[17] The causal factor in these situations is that leaders at the most senior levels have failed to articulate a "digital direction" that the workforce could embrace.

2. *Misaligned Goals.* If employees do not believe the new digital technology will help them to achieve their performance targets, then they will not use it. No matter how much executives drive a digital initiative it will go nowhere without an enrolled workforce. Employees will feign support and find workarounds that give them greater confidence. The causal factor is misaligned goals and performance targets. This occurs when the goals held at the top of the company for a digital transformation do not cascade throughout the organization and often conflict with the targets already established for the employees in their current roles. Employee targets need to be modified to reflect the new goals and there must be some transition time. Employees working toward X (which were the targets set for their rewards) will be reluctant to immediately switch to target Y if they believe all of their previous efforts toward X will be ignored.

Another misalignment can occur when employees are heavily invested in legacy systems and processes and are reluctant to embrace change. In this situation, employee behaviors can become a major roadblock. I, Leanne, was part of such a roadblock many years back when the first personal computers appeared at my workplace (a research and development organization). Employees had relied on secretaries to do all of the typing of papers and manuscripts. Hand-written copies were delivered to the secretaries who typed the documents and revised them as necessary with white-out where possible. One day, a personal computer was delivered to each employee's office. The expectation was that these new products would be embraced wholeheartedly as employees could now produce and revise their own documents. There were a few tech savvy employees who actually saw this as an opportunity, but for most of us it was seen as requiring us to do work that had previously been done by others. Needless to say, over time all had to embrace the new equipment and most of the secretaries had to learn new skills in addition to typing.

3. *Data Fatigue.* This was an issue for the industrial hardware operation described above. Digital systems generate immense data which is often at a level never seen before by an organization. It is inevitable. If the data is unused, it can create a burden for employees just in the matter of managing it. Often, the data creates a new level of transparency within an organization that can become threatening to employees who want to protect their turf. The causal factor is that executives have not provided the workforce with the freedom, flexibility, tools, standardized processes, and structures to use the data efficiently and effectively. This is an area where Honeywell excelled, and the results show it.[16]

## NELM: THE WAY FORWARD

The common pitfalls taken in context of the broad trends noted earlier paint a challenging picture of what it takes for *traditional enterprises* to remain competitive in the digital world. We have stated in our training programs and books that, "At the root cause level all success and failure is driven by leadership." Thus, we believe that our Nine Elements of Leadership Mastery (NELM) provide an excellent framework for an organization's digital undertaking. We will illustrate this belief in the following sections by walking through each of the nine Elements.

### Element 1: Set Direction

In *Becoming a Leader*, we established that setting direction for people and organizations is a leadership act of the highest importance because it meets a basic human need to be on a journey. We now extend this to an organization's digital journey.

A great deal of scholarly work has centered on the need for executives at the highest level to describe a vision and purpose, i.e., direction, for a digital strategy, but less attention has been paid to the style of leadership that makes this happen.[18] That's where NELM fills the gap.

Figure 7.1 illustrates the framework for Setting Direction that we developed in *Becoming a Leader*, modified slightly for a digital direction.

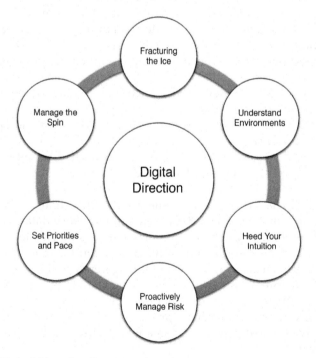

**Figure 7.1** Digital Direction Framework

### Fracturing the Ice

A digital direction begins with "fracturing your ice and the ice of others" especially at the highest levels in an organization (see Chapter 3). Change guru Kurt Lewin refers to this stage as unfreezing or the first stage of transition and one of the most critical stages in the entire process of change management. "It involves improving the readiness as well as the willingness of people to change by fostering a realization for moving from the existing comfort zone to a transformed situation. It involves making people aware of the need for change and improving their motivation for accepting the new ways of working for better results. During this stage, effective communication plays a vital role in getting the desired support and involvement of the people in the change process."[19]

CEOs and senior executives must have an understanding of how employees on the front-line work and how digital tools could make a difference, else they will push out unreasonable expectations.[20] Instead of top-down digital directives, executives need to "take inventory" of what has informed them about the possible use of digital tools in their company. They must demonstrate a willingness and ability to consider facts, knowledge, and what they believe about digital technology, as well has having a "trigger mechanism" to constantly challenge each. Ideally, this mechanism would also influence others in the organization, become a catalyst for change by accessing information, and establish and nurture relationships within the organization to socialize the information and anticipate key changes required for success.[18]

You might be thinking, "how do they do all of that?" It gets down to the way executives (and others) interact with people in the environment internal to the organization. We have long been advocates of Susan Scott's "Interrogating Reality" model and described it extensively in Chapter 3. Essentially, leaders stop issuing directives and replace them with proposals about digital initiatives. They intentionally invite others to share their knowledge and understanding which creates "fractures" in what people believe about the status quo and what digital has to offer. Everyone involved in the proposal learns, which triggers them to challenge the real potential of a digital undertaking. The learning is bidirectional – senior executives learn what the workforce needs, and the workforce learns what is possible with digital technology. When a web of digital proposals cascades throughout an organization the quality of the decision-making improves exponentially because people are better informed. And, misaligned goals and employee resistance (discussed above) is less of an issue. Moreover, an awareness of pivotal changes required within the organization emerges. These changes are not force-fed from the top but cascade up from the front line. In this way a genuine commitment to change emerges that, "harnesses the courage, imagination, patience, intelligence, and spirit of all people in the organization."[21]

An example will illustrate the point. I, Leanne, was part of a pivotal change required at one of the universities where I worked. A directive came from the university president's office that a human resources management system (PeopleSoft) was to be implemented and the goal was to have it done in record time. This impacted virtually every staff person in the organization. The presumption was that the president wanted this done in record time in order to demonstrate that it could be done, even though it was going to be extremely taxing to the staff to implement a radical change to every (integrated) personnel system in such a short time. As imagined, the directive was met with resistance and cynicism but the unrelenting pressure was moving it along. Near the end of its implementation the president made it known that the need for immediacy was because the payroll system was about to fail and unless it was updated as soon as feasible it was likely that people were not going to get paid (perhaps for some duration). Had this reason been known, which would have happened through a web of cascading proposals as described above, the buy-in would have been much different. Ironically, the president cloaked the true reason for urgency because he did not want to put people in fear of not getting paid – a fear that would have been addressed through the process of proposals.

### Understand Environments

So far, we have talked about establishing a digital vision and purpose by fracturing ice internally in an organization. But a "trigger mechanism" for the external environment is also critical. We described this mechanism in Chapter 3 as "a rigorous and purposeful relationship with the environments that influence our existence." An awareness of threats and opportunities can emerge from the identification of constraints that digital technologies impose on an organization's competitiveness. The industrial hardware example (above) illustrates this perfectly. The CEO realized that *born-digital* enterprises had shifted consumer expectations to value being able to view products online. This had become a constraint for his business because it lacked the ability to meet the needs of a tech-savvy and connected consumer. When he detected and acknowledged the constraint, he was able to do something about it. He confronted it by implementing an off-the-shelf web-based ordering system, responded by building a fulfillment center when online retail demand increased unexpectedly, and now plans to adapt his overall business model to include analytics.

Figure 3.4 in Chapter 3 illustrates the constraint framework: detect > confront > respond > adapt. In the end the industrial hardware enterprise COP'ed a viable future. Had the CEO not detected (or ignored) the constraint, his business would have been FUC'ed. But this is a short-term situation. Digital technology is disruptive continuously to any equilibrium,[18] internally and externally, and the cycle of fracturing ice, detecting constraints, responding, and adapting must be equally continuous in order to sustain viability. Digital technologists Michael Gale and Chris Aarons describe four drivers of continuous digital disruption:[22]

1. *"Supply and demand are compressing."* Born-digital companies like Amazon (Prime), Lyft, Uber, and Netflix have paved the way for a near-instant matching of demand to supply. For example, it is almost inconceivable that there was a time not long ago when people would drive to a video store to rent

movies on VHS or DVD and drive again to return them the next day. Now, movies are just a click away without leaving your couch.

2. *"Customers, partners, and employees have more information than ever before."* Social media and other internet services provide avenues of instant digital feedback about companies, their executives, employee concerns, product quality, customer complaints, etc.

3. *"The ability to scale is almost instant."* Cloud providers like Amazon, Apple, and Microsoft offer pay-as-you-go services and solutions. Off-the-shelf and customized analytics and AI capabilities are available from many consulting companies like Accenture, Blue Yonder, and Deloitte; and relatively inexpensive digital transformation training programs are offered by MIT, Berkeley, and other universities.[23]

4. *"Start-ups can threaten your segment."* According to Gale and Aarons, three new startups are launched every second – over 10,000 possible competitors per hour. A stunning statistic by any measure.

For *traditional enterprises*, these digital disruptors redefine "adapting" in our constraint framework to be more pervasive in scope. In other words, it can feel like a sledgehammer has come down on an organization. In addition to software and technology, adapting includes new methodologies, operational processes and procedures, project management, business models, mindsets, performance management, individual tasks, and even employees.[24] All of these adaptations mean people must behave differently and behavioral change is hard as we have noted many times in our writing.

### Heed Your Intuition

This brings us to the role of intuition. In *Becoming a Leader*, we talked about the dark side of data that comes to us in the form of analysis, charts, facts, assessments, and reports. The dark side being that data can blind us to seeing other realities and possibilities, which are particularly important when setting direction. This occurs because data is a form of observation and conclusions will be drawn in line with the data presented, and simultaneously preclude other conclusions had different data been observed. Economic models are a good example. Any economic model includes assumptions and a selection of predictors. In no case can every possible predictor be included, and the usefulness of the model is based on both the assumptions and the predictors chosen; thus, the importance of intuition as a supplement to data. We offer that leaders need to optimize their intuition using the following four-step process:

*Step 1:* Give yourself permission to listen to your intuition and to acknowledge that it is not just "gut feel" or emotion; rather it is a neurological process. Permit your consciousness to sense that a problem or opportunity exists.

*Step 2:* Be aware that you are vulnerable to being blinded by language, data, and passion, and influenced by observations – your own and those of others.

*Step 3:* Mentally "connect the dots" – like many pieces of exquisite art, you stand back and synthesize the data and your experience into an integrated picture of reality.

*Step 4:* Think about risks and identify feasible conclusions.

You might be thinking, "Has intuition been displaced by big data, AI, and machine learning?" It's a good question considering that a core value of digital technology is the capture of immense data that can be mined for efficiencies and learning.[19] Some experts believe that leaders need to reconsider the role of data in decision-making, relying on it more – and less on intuition.[19] We agree and disagree – clearly, we need to explain what we mean.

Box 7.1 describes how digital data and analytics have revolutionized *internal* and *external interfaces* including everything from medical services, production optimization, and advertising, to the choices a customer sees and selects from when ordering pizza on their mobile device. Data has become so valuable in decision-making that companies are fighting over who has access to it. For example, online advertising is built around access to huge amounts of data and, as of this writing, Apple and Facebook are going head-to-head over which company controls the data.[25] Advertisers target customers through their own sites, platforms on Facebook, and Apple's apps, matching them to Internet Protocol addresses (IP address), phone numbers, and the unique advertising identifiers built into mobile devices. Companies like Facebook create algorithms (discussed in Chapters 3 and 5) using AI to create "digital-twins" of potential audiences for an advertiser's products. These algorithms allow companies to target markets of people who have digital identities with a preference for a particular product.

We believe that digital data and analytics has altered Step 3 of our intuition optimization process. Specifically, it has created the ability to observe enormous amounts of data and "connect the dots" beyond what has been available mentally. (This is what is occurring with the advertisers noted above – the algorithms are gathering and connecting disparate information into a "look-alike" audience).

If anything, these new abilities have taken the role of intuition to an even higher level. Much like the Greek god Prometheus created humanity from clay, digital technology has created insights from previously unavailable and/ or disconnected data. The role of consciousness (Step 1), understanding one's vulnerability (Step 2), and awareness of risks (Step 4) has only become more important (not less) in decision-making. Leaders need to be diligent in understanding that all digital data is past-oriented and will always have limits in predicting future possibilities and risks. Just because we have more data, more analytics, more simulations, and more machine learning does not mean that we have a lock on future realities and possibilities. Clearly, optimizing one's intuition is even as (if not more) critical in the digital age.

### *Proactively Manage Risk*

So far in this chapter we have described ten potential risks occurring from trends, pitfalls, and disruptors either as a result of or concurrent with digital technology:

*Trends*

1. Greater prospect of surprises
2. Greater prospect of interdependencies
3. Greater prospect of obsolescence

*Pitfalls*

4. Hierarchy myopia
5. Misaligned goals
6. Data fatigue

*Disruptors*

7. Supply and demand are compressing
8. Customers, partners, and employees have more information than ever before
9. The ability to scale is almost instant
10. Start-ups can threaten your segment.

These risks are in addition to the plethora of other risks that can occur from human error, mechanical or process failures, adverse government or political actions, and loss of competitive advantage. GM and Ford idling manufacturing facilities due to semiconductor shortages and a giant container ship wedged across the Suez Canal for a week (blocking nearly $10 billion each day in global trade) are just two reminders at the time of this writing of the ever-present and damaging potential of unforeseen risk events.

In *Becoming a Leader* we advanced the risk management methodology (RMM) shown in Figure 7.2 for being proactive with risk management. It includes (a) identify potential risk events (e.g. startups threatening your segment), (b) quantify the impact if the event occurs, (c) evaluate the current capacity – employee skills, processes, and structures – to manage the consequences of the events, and (d) assess the likelihood that the event will occur. Risks with the highest probable impact and lowest manageability are considered critical. Being proactive involves consideration of (a) – (d) plus (e) taking actions and deploying resources to either eliminate the risk or improve manageability in the event of occurrence. Essentially, you are thinking about what could go wrong today, tomorrow, a year from now, ten years from now, and you're managing the risks. Referring back to Chapter 3, Figure 3.1 The Journey, you are looking for risks all the way down the road and from side to side.

Much like intuition, digital technology only elevates the need for risk management. Clearly, in examples described above (Suncor, Honeywell, Industrial Hardware, and GE), risk management was key to the actions these companies put in place, some more successful than others.

Another consideration is that we actually want employees to take on more risk with digital initiatives, but the risk management must be rigorous.

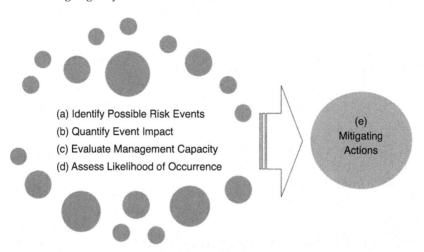

**Figure 7.2** Risk Management Methodology (RMM)

As we will develop later, for a successful digital transformation, employees must experiment with the technologies, learn from successes and failures, and steward the agility required for their teams to adapt in some cases and innovate in others. If RMM does not occur or is not widely practiced at all levels in an organization, employees will lack the psychological safety (See Chapter 4) to experiment, and the digital direction will fail, no matter how hard it is driven by management.

### Set Priorities and Pace

In Chapter 4 we discussed stress in its good and bad forms. Bad stress – called distress – occurs when something causes emotional pressure for an extended period of time, or if short in duration, we perceive it to have negative consequences for us personally. Data fatigue as noted above is an example of something that can cause distress, especially if there is a feeling of little or no control. Equally, distress can occur when a digital transformation goal is set for an organization without defining clear priorities (i.e., this first, then that second) or if the digital initiatives are not paced in line with the organization's capacity to deliver them.

People and organizations in distress will fail – it is that simple – because the health of employees and teams will decline, leading to fight-or-flight behavior.

A leader's job in a digital transformation is to help employees with priorities and to shape expectations about the relative importance of planned actions. We recommend the following steps:

1. Focus on digital goals derived from "fracturing ice" and understanding of internal and external constraints as described above.

2. Prioritize these into three or four critical goals by using risk analysis (RMM), intuition, and other critical information.
3. Define clear and realistic timelines consistent with available resources (people skills and capital)
4. Assign specific accountabilities to individuals and teams.
5. Review and update steps 1–4 often. This will ensure agility as the goals and execution plans require adjustment over time as environments shift.

In performing steps 1 and 2, research indicates that leaders should focus initially on "hard to reverse" choices that are critical for the organization's success.[26] In clarifying steps 3 and 4 for these choices, an approach inevitably will be tested and perfected within the organization for handling all other digital initiatives. There surely will be false starts. A client in the engineering, procurement, and construction industry described a situation that occurred when this approach was not followed.

> We started with the easy stuff first, the quick "digital wins," and now we have a piecemealed mess with operational, project management, and enterprise systems in a data gridlock … we had to put together a "lean team" just to clean up the mess … we would have been better off starting with the hard choices first.

Another consideration in setting priorities is identifying and then eliminating processes, practices, and structures (PPSs) that will be supplanted by the digital investments. The targeted PPSs could range from major enterprise systems to meeting frequencies, project review protocols, employee roles and responsibilities, etc. A company's use of digital technology for virtual meetings (Zoom, Starleaf, and Microsoft Teams, to name a few) during the COVID-19 pandemic is a good example. It replaced travel for face-to-face meetings and all functions (i.e., PPSs) associated with arranging and executing travel were suspended and in some cases eliminated entirely.

By signaling an intent to eliminate the PPSs early on, leaders send clear messages to employees about the organization's commitment to change – thus reducing the risk of distress.[27] Fear of the unknown can be a major stressor in an organization and early messaging from leaders, especially executives, is critical.

### Manage the Spin

This brings us to the final task in setting a digital direction – managing the spin. Leaders must communicate a digital direction to everyone in the organization (and outside too) in a way that creates energy, enthusiasm, and commitment for change. There is a role for well-defined vision and mission statements, but it has been our experience that sound bites resonate more pervasively and powerfully in an organization – going beyond rhetoric – and shaping awareness among employees of how changes matter to them in fulfilling their jobs.

Without these sound bites provided by leaders, especially CEOs and senior executives, the workforce (and customers) will invent a spin and it will not be helpful.

A good spin is communicated verbally in less than 60 seconds. Here are the questions to answer with sound bites that shape healthy spin for a digital direction:

- Where are we going with the digital undertaking?
- Why are we going there?
- Who is going with us?
- What specifically are we going to do?
- When will the undertaking have effect?

How these questions are answered depends on each organization's unique situation. One rule of thumb is to answer them at least one or two levels beyond (bigger than) your digital undertaking. For example, Nike's digital vision is not about selling shoes; it wants to be a part of its customers lives,[28] and CVS's drive is to be a health care company with digital woven into pharmacies, retail stores, and health clinics.[29]

Recall the retail–industrial hardware from the beginning of the chapter? The CEO bought an off-the-shelf web-based ordering system and then built a new facility for replenishment and online order fulfillment. Here is an example of how the CEO could spin the digital undertaking:

*We are in pursuit of purposeful business relationships*

*with current and future customers and partners,*

*as a means to confront marketing and sales constraints*

*that are holding us back from achieving our fullest potential.*

*To this end, we will invest in the digital tools*

*that our employees need – to be informed about – and to meet customer expectations.*

*Our plan is to have this new technology in place by year's end.*

Notice how the spin answers the key questions:

- Where are we going with the digital undertaking? *We are in pursuit of purposeful business relationships.*
- Why are we going there? *Means to confront marketing and sales constraints that are holding us back from achieving our fullest potential.*
- Who is going with us? *Employees; current and future customers and partners.*
- What specifically are we going to do? *Invest in digital tools that our employees need – to be informed about – and meet customer expectations.*
- When will the undertaking have effect? *Our plan is to have this new technology in place by year's end.*

Imagine if the university president described earlier would have had a spin like this for the PeopleSoft conversion. Employee reactions likely would have been hugely more positive.

### Element 2: Build Teams of People

In *Becoming a Leader* we went to considerable length in explaining the two leadership tasks in team development. These tasks are even more critical for teams directly and/or tangentially involved in digital undertakings.

   *1. Seek Cognitive and Demographic Diversity.* A digital initiative will be far more successful with teams of non-like-minded individuals with diverse demographic backgrounds and cognitive functions (see Box 7.2). The hazards of poor diversity – Groupthink and conformity – can be serious problems when attempting to implement digital changes. Teams involved in digital projects need a lot of diverse opinions in order to avoid homogeneous thinking and to create innovative and inclusive digital solutions.[18]

   *2. Nurture Teams to High Performance.* Leaders must be diligent during digital undertakings to:

- Encourage constructive conversations.
- Ensure the digital direction is widely understood.
- Intervene and coach when signals suggest members' behavior may be deteriorating.
- Ask questions that evoke insights and highlight problem areas.
- Inspire others by being vulnerable with insecurities or concerns about experimenting with new ideas and risk-taking – essential to establish a psychologically safe environment.

In addition, leaders must be effective in confronting the inevitable conflicts that will occur during a digital transition. A Veritas Conversation (explained in Chapter 1 and in more detail in *Becoming a Leader*) is an essential tool for mitigating conflict within teams.

---

## Box 7.2:  Demographic and Cognitive Diversity: Differentiators

| Demographic | Cognitive |
|---|---|
| Gender | Observations |
| Race | Viewpoints |
| Religion | Processing Style |
| Ethnicity | Problem Solving Style |
| Age | Threat Awareness |
| Socioeconomic | Feelings/Emotions |

---

   There is research that suggests *traditional enterprises* (considering digital undertakings) should punctuate existing teams with new hires having digital and/or e-commerce background, and then teach them the specifics about the business.[29] These new hires could kickstart the digital effort, especially if they have "a track record of producing digital products with measurable value" and "the ability to enable and systematize into the organization a new way of thinking and doing."[30] Among existing employees, we need to be careful in selecting for digital projects those with "headroom" for growth (discussed later in Element 8). These are not just the "usual suspects" (see Chapter 4) with proven skills, but also those who would benefit from the experience and could increase their value to the organization going forward.

## Element 3: Create Key Processes

For those who have not read our earlier books, we categorize processes into two buckets: (1) enterprise processes, which we call the domain of managers, and these include most of the ways things get done in an organization, and (2) leadership processes which we define as assurance, performance management, and rewards. The latter processes enable and support the managers and teams within the organization. Both buckets can be the center of a digital undertaking, but enterprise processes tend to be more leveraging (and get most attention) for digital technologies because these cover most *external interfaces* and *internal structures and processes*. Leadership processes are often overlooked. For the purpose of this writing, i.e., leadership, we will focus on a handful of assurance, performance management, and rewards issues critical for successful digital investments.

### *Manage the Messages*

As mentioned in the section above, Set Priorities and Pace, leaders must send clear messages to employees about the intent of digital initiatives. This can be difficult when it comes to how initiatives will be assessed in terms of performance delivery and how employees will be rewarded (or not) for success (or failure). The messages are often blurred by the challenges of understanding and implementing the technologies. Interestingly, the specifics about the various digital projects, which we call *content*, are often clear, but the objectives and the situational aspects, or *context*, can get lost in an organization. When this occurs, employees will bring their own *context* to bear (as occurred with the university employees during the PeopleSoft conversion), and that might drive the wrong messages about management's intention, often creating a toxic culture in an organization as noted in the previous chapter. This is why the spin, discussed above, is absolutely critical. The spin brings the *context* to life by answering the five questions – where, why, who, what, and when?

During a digital undertaking, the spin must be spoken loudly and often in an organization, cascading down and out. Leaders would do well to keep the following formula in mind: *Message = Content + Context*, and remember that their job is to supply both.

## The System: Goals>Metrics>Measures>Targets

We have referred to this performance management system many times in this book. Organizations must have goals, goals must have metrics, which must have measures, and these must have targets. This principle applies to all digital undertakings. To illustrate the connection, here is how the retail–industrial hardware could use the system:

- **Goals** – *What are we going to do?* Confront competitor pressure in existing and potential markets.
- **Metrics –** *How will we do it?*
  ○ Install a web-based online access and ordering system
  ○ Build a new fulfillment center for online sales
- **Measures** – *How will it be measured?*
  ○ *Capital Investment*
  ○ *Employee Additions*
  ○ *Net Revenue Growth*
- **Targets** – *What is the target?*
  ○ *Capital Investment* not to exceed $650,000
  ○ *Employee additions* not to exceed 60 full-time equivalent (FTE)
  ○ *Net Revenue Growth* greater than 30 percent by year three.

There are a couple things to point out with this example. First, the goal is defined as bigger than the digital investment. Meaning, the business goal – confronting competitive pressure – is the imperative and the digital investment is one of the ways it is achieved. It is important to have all digital investments described in terms of a business imperative, else the justification and purpose become lost. Moreover, a bigger goal is like an "envelope" that attracts and invites innovation associated with learning and experimentation. This is clear with the retail–industrial hardware. It started out purchasing an off-the-shelf system and soon saw the tangential opportunity to add a new facility to handle growing online sales. Once the analytics capability is achieved, they may see other digital opportunities for efficiencies and logistics in the new facility.

It is also noteworthy that the system creates a 'balanced scorecard" for the undertaking. The zone of attention is on both costs and revenue, thus keeping accountable people focused on enabling tasks while not losing sight of the purpose of the undertaking. Special care should be taken to ensure that everyone involved in a digital project understands the performance goals>-metrics>measures>targets. Performance must be transparent at all levels, sharing information as broadly as possible.

Digital investments should not be justified by "becoming digital," rather they must improve the profitability and/or viability of the organization. There is often a lot of hype and overselling from digital suppliers[31] which can make it difficult to nail down measures and targets. Our view is – if you cannot determine how to measure the benefits of a digital investment then you probably should not make it until you can. One of our "laws of performance management" states, *if you can't measure it, you can't manage it … if you don't measure it, it won't be managed*. The career graveyards are loaded with former managers and executives who lost sight of this law.

### Assurance Monitoring

A key milestone in a digital undertaking occurs when a leader delegates authority and responsibility to a team or individual for the delivery of a project. The system described above will form the basis of a contract between the parties under which accountable people promise to deliver the targets and the leader promises to support, delegate authority to act, and otherwise help in the delivery. The leader's job is just beginning at this point.

Ongoing performance monitoring by the leader is critical. Technology projects are notorious for scope creep, cost expansion, and delays. Given the web of connectivity associated with most technology systems, the risk of unawareness or hidden information at the time of decision-making is high, and further complications can emerge from unknown future information and factors. Reviewing data and progress reports is one thing, but not a substitute for a leader engaging individuals and project teams in regular conversations about the project. Interventions may be required during a project's cycle, and a conversation can create the awareness – of issues and opportunities – and help the accountable people manage through these. There is no lonelier moment in a person's career than when they find themselves in trouble with a project and no one to look to for support.

Monitoring conversations are also important because we want people to experiment and take managed risks with digital projects. There will be incremental wins and failures – it is inevitable – and a fear of failure can be a roadblock to learning. Learning from things that went wrong is key and is frequently the catalyst for innovation. This is called "failing forward."[30] Conversations between leaders and accountable team members create the safe landing cushion for failing forward.

### Rewards

We advocate team bonuses for digital undertakings that are additive to base pay and tied directly to the targets set forth in the balanced score card. This way there is a clear alignment between the organization's goals and those of the individuals. Moreover, a bonus element can reward teamwork which is nearly always critical for a digital project.

As we described in *Becoming a Leader*, a leader is often faced with the dilemma of an individual or team that tried hard, and showed considerable commitment to a goal, but failed to deliver the target. The question is, do they suffer the consequences of a failure? Yes, is the answer. However, in these situations a leader will consider the following in making a judgment about consequences:

- The quality of the interventions, i.e., did the individual or team take corrective actions when they observed, or should have observed, that a problem emerged.

- The accountable person's understanding of the risks inherent in the environment and the contingency planning reflected in the project design and process decisions.
- New ideas generated, and opportunities identified from following test-and-learn practices.

Regarding the last bullet, spot awards also can be used for individuals who put forth special effort that drives innovation and new digital opportunities, particularly when the project achieved less-than-expected results. By using spot awards, management is acknowledging the effort and encouraging that the behavior is repeated.

### Element 4: Steward Structure

We mentioned above that "scope creep" often occurs with technology projects. This is especially true for digital projects. A good performance management system and assurance monitoring will help mitigate the creep, but one might ask why it exists in the first place. To the best of our knowledge there is no law in physics that explains this. Our belief is that an improper structure is the root cause, and it manifests itself in one or all of the *five failure factors* described in Box 7.3.

---

## Box 7.3:  Digital Project Scope Creep: Five Failure Factors

1. Improper or inadequate analysis of the original scope.
2. Poor communication between the users of the digital technology and the individuals or teams managing the project.
3. Misaligned authority delegation and responsibility resulting in a lack of or blurred accountability.
4. Overwhelming plethora of digital offerings from aggressive suppliers resulting in a company selecting a digital product that does not integrate with its existing systems.
5. Unclear protocol for design changes.

---

A case in point is GE's digital undertaking discussed earlier. According to former executives at GE Digital and corporate headquarters, the project was wasteful because huge amounts of money and people were poured into product development "without a coherent strategy and well-thought-out process."[17] In hindsight, these executives believe that GE should have put together a small team to identify and evaluate options and risks before hiring armies of new employees and promoting yet-to-be designed products to potential customers.[17] Interestingly, if you look back at Figure 7.1 Digital Direction Framework, you can readily see that had GE followed the framework it likely would have had a better initial outcome.

Thus, we believe that organizations, especially *traditional enterprises*, should use an initiative structure to steward the Framework for at least the first 100 days of a digital undertaking. Specifically, we call this a Digital Initiative Team (DIT) and it has an *on-the-field* structure and an *ad hoc process* as explained below.

### *Digital Initiative Team (DIT):* **On-the-Field Structure**

We use the sports metaphor *on the field* in contrast to *in the stands* to make the distinction between those who observe and critique what others do versus those who are doing *the doing*, i.e., in action, committed to direction, learning, adapting, and responding to feedback. Successfully implementing a Digital Direction Framework is not going to happen through the normal channels in most organizations. Thus, special resources and people must be focused on it.

Our *on-the-field* structure is illustrated in Figure 7.3. It is a temporary structure in that its initial term of existence is for 100 days.

### *Steering Committee*

A top priority is establishing a steering committee at the outset and appointing a chairman who serves as the champion of the entire effort. The committee is primarily a decision-making body. But it also cajoles and smooths the way for having buy-in and alignment when dealing with inevitably difficult issues.

The committee owns the digital initiative, i.e., the members are accountable and have the responsibility and commensurate delegated authority for

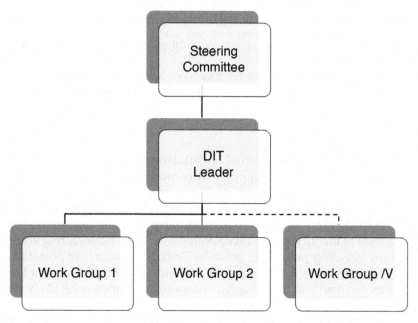

**Figure 7.3** DIT On-the-Field Structure

all decision-making in the 100-day period. Research has shown that clarifying accountability for digital initiatives is key as it is often "hotly contested" and a source of considerable angst as resources are prioritized and decisions are made that could change many parts (if not all) of an organization.[32]

The level of the chairman in the organization depends on what is being considered but our recommendation is the chairman should be as highly placed as possible. In many organizations the chairman should be the CEO because of the significant decisions that likely will be made by the committee.

Members of the committee should be executives or senior managers from areas of the organization that could be affected by digital technology. Enterprise-wide representation is essential as digital initiatives can cut across business strategies, and not be centered on just IT (Information Technology), often morphing into a "digital business strategy."[33] We want this group to surface and deal with the many disputes, disagreements, and challenges that are likely. As noted in Chapter 2 about Machiavelli, it is the avoidance of confrontations that makes challengers bolder. This group confronts tensions so they do not fester at lower levels in the organization where they can subvert goals and undermine the success of the digital undertaking.

This means that the committee members must be aligned themselves and any tensions among them must be worked out before the ad hoc process begins (discussed below). Using an analogy from Chapter 6, imagine that the committee is the spine of the organization and individually each is a vertebrae. "If any one of them is out of line you've got massive pressure on the nerves and then pain all the way up and down the spinal column."[34] A weak backbone is certain failure for a digital initiative.

We noted earlier that digital technology leads to the capture of immense data that can be mined for efficiencies (and learning) that ultimately cause the supplantation of some existing processes, practices, and structures (PPSs). Employee roles and responsibilities also will change as data control becomes less siloed and new internal networks emerge around shared data.[20] The committee is critical for managing and sending clear messages to employees about the organization's commitment to change. As noted earlier, fear of the unknown can be a major stressor in an organization and messaging from the committee is critical.

## DIT Leader

Also critical is the selection of the DIT Leader. This is a full-time position that "wears" many hats: strategist, counselor, coach, team builder, arm-twister, coordinator, and budget controller. You might be thinking that the DIT Leader should come from the IT unit. IT expertise needs to be deployed in the working groups (discussed next), but the leader of the initiative can come from any part of an organization. He or she must be familiar with digital technology but not necessarily an expert. It is more important that the person has sufficient expertise in cross-enterprise, cross-functional projects, and the ability to lead networks of people and teams rather than relying on hierarchy.[30]

High emotional intelligence and Versatility (See Chapter 5) are essential, as are personality preferences for energy derived from interactions with people (Extraversion), ability to see patterns and connections (Intuition) and a flexible and adaptable worldview (Perceiver). See Chapter 2 in *Becoming a Leader* for a review of personality preferences.

### Work Groups

The DIT Leader reaches out into the organization to form the work groups. Much like the steering committee, the work groups must have enterprise-wide representation. A work group should be assembled for each function and business unit (or segment thereof) that could be affected by digital technology. The members of the groups are drawn from their respective units. These people should not include those who are merely available, but must be those with skills, expertise, information, relationships, and support in their units. These groups should also have digital expertise drawn from within the IT unit or external digital consultants as appropriate. Normally, work group members retain their full-time positions but are provided time to participate in the digital initiative. This way they maintain the vital link to their unit's day-to-day operations.

The job of the work groups, in the first instance, is to map out the digital possibilities for their respective units. They do this by interfacing with employees in their units on the front-line who can imagine whether and how digital tools could make a difference in their jobs. The work groups should be coached on how to have these conversations. The focus needs to shift from problem description and on to "what's possible." Problems are past-oriented and carry with them a degree of organizational guilt and blame. A work group will be blinded to the true digital possibilities if all they do is focus on fixing past problems, especially if some of the members feel the weight of guilt or blame.

At this point, we want to refer back to our discussion about Fracturing the Ice in Figure 7.1. The *on-the-field* structure is the architecture by which executives "take inventory" of the possible use of digital tools in their company, and therewith challenge their understanding of digital applications. This architecture connects employees on the front line directly to the decision-makers at executive levels of the company. Instead of top-down or forced-fed directives, the structure enables an *ad hoc process* that drives a two-way "trigger mechanism" that unearths a truly viable digital direction. The process by itself becomes the desired catalyst for change that (sorry for the repeat), "harnesses the courage, imagination, patience, intelligence, and spirit of all people in the organization."[21]

### Digital Initiative Team (DIT): Ad Hoc Process

Figure 7.4 illustrates the ad hoc process. We use the words *ad hoc* because the process has the singular purpose of implementing the Digital Direction Framework within 100 days, and then it ends.

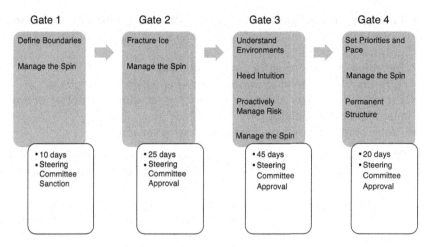

**Figure 7.4** DIT Ad Hoc Process

We have borrowed a phase–gate practice commonly used in project management to control risks, monitor scope changes, and maintain stakeholder interest.[35] Our objective is to manage and control the five failure factors for digital projects described earlier in Box 7.3.

Essentially, the process centers on conversations among stakeholders. As we describe below, conversations are required to open a gate and to close it once it has been confirmed that the desired goals have been achieved.

## Stage Gate 1

In this stage, the DIT Leader prepares and proposes to the steering committee a set of boundaries for the digital initiative. This is a difficult task as there are no clear guidelines. If the boundaries are too broad the initiative could lose focus; too narrow and possibilities could be missed. For example, a societal initiative to increase protein levels in diets of poor nations might get something accomplished, while one to solve world hunger would struggle to meet its goal. Our recommendation is to err on being too narrow as the boundaries tend to expand through discovery during the initiative. Some general categories of boundaries include:

- Internal structures and processes to drive efficiency, cost savings, and simplify work processes.
- External interfaces to meet evolving preferences of current and potential customers.
- Current business model.
- Potential and new business models.
- Machine learning, digital twins, and AI applications.
- Preferred digital technology suppliers.
- Use of external digital consultants.

- Functions and business units selected for work group representation.
- Criteria for selection of work group members (e.g., cognitive and demographic diversity)
- Incentive awards for work group members.
- Training for the steering committee and work group members.
- Protocol for review and approval by the steering committee of subsequent boundary changes.
- Protocol for approval of stage-gate time extensions.

The DIT Leader also prepares the spin for the digital initiative. The spin describes the structure and process of the initiative and answers the questions: where, why, who, what, and when. The objective is to provide the content and context that employees need in order to get the right messages about the initiative. As we have noted many times, without context from management, the workforce will bring their own context to bear and derive messages that could be unhelpful. The worst outcome would be perceived messages that cause distress and cannibalize the health, energy, and enthusiasm of the workforce.

The spin is updated for Gates 2 and 3 in order to keep the workforce informed of progress, again trying to manage messaging.

The DIT Leader uses every resource available to prepare the boundaries and spin and presents them to the steering committee. The chairman facilitates a review conversation among the steering committee members. Typically, approval must be unanimous in order to move to the next stage.

## Stage Gate 2

In this stage, the work groups are mobilized as a network of digital "proposers" to the targeted functions and business units. They push out and invite the sharing of knowledge with the front-line workforce about digital capabilities. This is entirely conversational. The work product is a listing or mapping of digital possibilities proposed by the units. Note the two-way functionality: work groups propose digital capabilities, and the units propose possibilities to apply those capabilities.

Here is an example. Imagine that a large hospital chain is considering a cost-saving investment to consolidate and store patient records in a digital format. Work groups could propose the digital undertaking to the hospital units and the doctors and medical staff in these units might propose that digital twins of patients be developed as algorithms to improve monitoring and doctor decision-making. In this case, what was proposed as a cost-saving initiative now has the possibility of improving patient care.

It is critical that the possibilities come from employees in the units and not from the work group members. (Hopefully, co-creation will occur through the conversations.) Ownership by employees in the units that will use the digital tools is a key factor for the success of a digital initiative.

At this point the possibilities are conceptual. The DIT Leader assembles and presents the "possibilities map" to the steering committee (along with the updated spin). During this review, the steering committee members become better informed about the applicability of digital technology in their organization, often seeing opportunities that were not previously visible to them. This is an important step because this knowledge causes them to challenge their own beliefs and makes them better able to exercise judgement.

It is not unusual for a steering group to redefine the initiative's boundaries at this stage. They could broaden them and in this case the timeline for the remaining gates may need to be revised. Normally, however, the decision is to narrow the map to the possibilities that appear to offer the greatest promise. These get passed to the next stage upon unanimous approval by the steering committee members. The conversations among the steering committee members to achieve this approval level is essential. The chairman's role is to facilitate the conversations to ensure that voices are heard, and a thorough consideration of the possibilities occurs. Arbitrating disputes and disagreements among the members is part of the job. It is likely that the members will have preferences for digital resources to be allocated to their own functions or business units. The goal is to advance the possibilities that are best for the overall enterprise, and that may take some compromising by individual members. The chairman may need to coach some members to get to this point.

### Stage Gate 3

We call this the "conversion stage." The approved possibilities from Gate 2 are passed back to the work groups with an objective to convert the possibilities to "probabilities" that can be implemented. They do this by rigorous analysis of the organization's internal and external environments (detect constraints > confront > respond > adapt), rigorous application of intuition (Steps 1–4), and a rigorous analysis of risks using the RMM discussed earlier. Those possibilities that prove probable given these analyses then get costed in terms of estimated investment dollars and people resources. It is at this point that initial benefits are established for each possibility and defined in terms of goals>metrics>measures>targets.

As discussed earlier in Element 3, only those possibilities with measurable benefits meet the test for conversion to probabilities. The assurance role of the DIT Leader at this stage cannot be overstated. Often, he or she will push back on the work groups and challenge them on the benefit determination. Clarity about how proposed digital tools do or do not integrate with existing systems is vital. I, Al, having been in a similar role in my career, can attest to the tenacity required to assure due diligence. It is not uncommon for several iterations to occur with the work groups before realistic benefits are quantified.

The DIT Leader presents the digital probabilities to the steering committee for consideration (along with the updated spin). The roles of the committee members and chairman are the same as Gate 2. The objective is to advance those probabilities to the final stage that offer the most promise for the organization, but this time the available investment dollars and people resources become a key part of the deliberation.

## Stage Gate 4

This is the "implementation plan" stage. The approved probabilities are passed back to the work groups to propose *priorities and pace* (Steps 1–4) as described in Element 1. Full project descriptions are prepared with particular attention to the "hard to reverse" choices. The estimates in Gate 3 for investment dollars, people resources, and benefits are now refined to high certainty levels. PPSs (processes, practices, and structures) that likely would be eliminated by the digital tools are identified. And contracts with digital suppliers are negotiated.

The DIT Leader compiles the information and completes a final prioritization and pacing for the overall list of projects. The due diligence role of the DIT Leader is again critical.

The DIT Leader also prepares the final spin, this time for the implementation plan which, as explained earlier, should be described as bigger than the digital investment. The spin answers the questions – where, why, who, what, and when – for the implementation of the digital program, with the objective of resonating pervasively and powerfully throughout the organization. Special attention is paid to the PPSs as these affect people directly through their roles and responsibilities. The spin will also declare the closure of the 100-day initiative and the handover of the implementation to a permanent structure for implementation.

The implementation plan and spin are then presented to the steering committee for review and approval. It is often the case that attractive projects will not make the final cut given the limits of available resources. As noted earlier, digital initiatives must be paced in line with an organization's capacity to deliver them. Disputes among members jockeying for their unit's interests are likely. The chairman's roles of facilitator, arbiter, and coach are especially important in this allocation of resources. The final outcome is an approved digital investment implementation plan.

## Handover to the Permanent Structure

The steering committee's final job is to set in place the permanent structure for implementation of the digital investments. This can be contentious as there are few guidelines available. The typical preference is to turn the implementation over to the existing organization where that IT function has a technical coordination and assurance role; other functions and business units implement the digital tools within their normal structure and management processes. Doing otherwise might lead to the decoupling of authority from those responsible for normal business delivery. The worry is than an entire organization can feel disenfranchised and step back from accountability.

Some organizations have put in place entire digital functions (Digital Unit) as a permanent structure. In this case the DIT Leader might become the Chief Digital Officer (CDO) and members of the work groups would return to their original unit roles but become matrixed with the Digital Unit. Being matrixed means they report to the CDO for all digital functionality and to their normal units for delivery and performance management. There is research that suggests this structure harnesses the drive and energy needed to be sufficiently nimble and agile for viability in a rapidly shifting digital world that is continuously disruptive. It also supports the cross-functional collaboration required to sustain a constant awareness of digital constraints (detect > confront > respond > adapt). One of our clients with a large digital agenda created a Digital Unit and held it in place for several years, and then redeployed it into the business units with a small digital team remaining in the IT group. This team drove the creation of several DITs in the ensuing years (Step 5 in Set Priorities and Pace).

The handover to a permanent structure can also result in even more transformational changes as we saw with Honeywell and GE, where entire businesses were formed to capture emerging market opportunities for which these companies had grown the digital capacity to be competitive.

## Element 5: Behaviors

Let us pause for a moment and think about where we are in the discussion of digital maturity in traditional enterprises. We have described a Digital Direction Framework that addresses the trends, pitfalls, and disruptors associated with digital technology. This framework ultimately leads to the identification of viable digital opportunities for an organization. We presented the need for cognitive and demographic diversity in teams working digital initiatives. A leader's role in nurturing these teams to high performance was outlined, as were the processes for messaging, performance management, assurance monitoring, and rewards. Lastly, we explained the factors that cause digital undertakings to fail, and we presented a temporary structure and an ad hoc process that minimizes (hopefully eliminates) the occurrence of these factors. We ended with the handover of an approved, funded, and fully resourced digital investment program to the permanent structure within the organization for implementation.

It is readily apparent at this point that leader and employee behaviors are laced throughout all of this. In fact, research has shown that behaviors are at the heart of success (and failure) in a digital undertaking.[28,29] We saw how inappropriate behavior at GE (*fake and bake*) undermined a CEO's ambitious efforts to embrace digital technology, and we highlighted how fight-or-flight behavior can occur when distressed employees attempt to protect legacy systems. The Digital Direction Framework and the Digital Initiative Team are designed to abate behavioral issues and nurture constructive behaviors in an organization as it progresses in digital maturity.

So, you might be wondering what are the important behaviors for the steering committee, DIT Leader, work group members, and people they interact with in the organization? Should you be looking for these behaviors to provide assurance (or cause for concern if not observed)? These are discussed below:

- *Collaboration.* A willingness to put oneself in service of colleagues and customers, and bridge across the formal organization and informal networks.[36] A foundation requirement for nurturing teams to high performance.

- *Compassion.* The ability to understand the emotional makeup of colleagues and customers (empathy) and to treat them according to their emotional needs by using a rational decision-making process that considers happiness, thriving, and suffering.
- *Versatility.* Described in Chapter 5. Managing one's energy for the situation, rather than being trapped or trapping others in stereotypes; and where a full expression of preferences by others is not only tolerated but encouraged. Absolute requirement for the DIT Leader. Also critical for those involved in AI and digital twins – which have had serious issues with ethics and discrimination.[37]
- *Vulnerability.* A willingness to ask for help, admit when worried, and apologize when wrong. Essential for building trust with colleagues and customers and for *fracturing the ice.*
- *Integrity.* Standing for something, having core values that are considered acceptable within the organization, and never being ambiguous or neutral about them. Also an imperative for building trust.
- *Motivation.* Displaying a passion for work (and imbuing in others) for reasons that go beyond money or status; a propensity to pursue goals with energy and persistence; relentless questions about "why"; enthusiasm for change and innovation, and an orientation towards delivery. A key ingredient for learning in general, especially from mistakes and "failing forward."
- *Adaptability.* Open to change and willingness to replenish perspectives and knowledge stores through continuing education, in-house training, cross-generational and reverse-mentoring programs.[29] Self-awareness and self-control (i.e., emotional intelligence) are key components important for being COP'ed in a digital world rather than FUC'ed.
- *Courage.* Willingness to take action or make decisions that comes from a deep understanding of the "regrets" of indecisiveness and delay. Essential for experimentation with digital technologies, risk taking, and the agility that they engender. A client once stated, "Our digital transformation really took off the day our CEO found the courage to commit to it."

Behaviors tend to become socialized and then systemic in an organization's culture to such an extent that it is difficult for leaders and employees to differentiate good from bad. This is why we advocate that owners of organizations or the directors who represent them become actively involved in oversight of an organization's culture (see Chapter 3).

To the extent that behavior gaps exist when considering a digital undertaking, strict adherence to the design of the Digital Direction Framework and the Digital Initiative Team becomes increasingly important. Healthy behaviors, on the other hand, open the door for greater flexibility.

## Element 6: Conversations

Are conversations less important in organizations because of the automated mining of vast amounts of data, machine learning, and AI? We queried the same in the earlier discussion about intuition. It is a fair question since most of the new digital functionality requires little human involvement. Adam Miner, a clinical psychologist at the Stanford School of Medicine recently stated,

> ... *an AI system can recall all of Wikipedia in seconds. For raw processing power and memory, it isn't even a contest between humans and AI systems, however ... things humans do without effort in conversations are currently beyond the most powerful AI system.*[38]

Digital technology is not about replacing human conversations; it actually makes them more important, just like we concluded for intuition. The real potential of digital technology lies in the realm of possibility and that requires connections among humans. Through these connections, leaders become "sense-makers"[39] by sharing the context essential for interpreting content via the exercise of judgment. Leaders make sense in the digital world through conversations with employees, customers, and experts that open doors for new possibilities.

As we discussed in Chapter 5 (and extensively in *Becoming a Leader*), humans influence each other's behavior and thought processes during conversations through neurological processes called "attuned relating" and "mirroring." Often the effect is beyond our conscious perception. The mental activity of others is interconnected during conversations from the sharing of goals and thoughts, and we "catch" emotions from others. This is how possibilities are co-created by participants during conversations.

The role of conversations in digital undertakings is compelling when we reflect on the many applications already mentioned in this chapter:

- The driver of shifts that occur in Leadership Zones of executives when they see the transformational opportunities of digital technologies.
- As a causal factor in failed digital initiatives when leaders do not articulate a "digital direction" that the workforce can embrace.
- The means by which leaders provide context and send clear messages to the workforce about the intent of digital initiatives.
- The medium by which leaders "fracture ice" when directives are replaced with proposals.
- When leaders confront inevitable conflicts using a Veritas Conversation, mitigating tensions so they do not fester and subvert digital goals.
- An important part of performance management when leaders engage in monitoring conversations with employees and provide a safe landing cushion for "failing forward."
- When the steering committee cajoles and smooths the way for buy-in and alignment.

- The main tool of the DIT Leader as he or she strategizes, counsels, coaches, arm twists, coordinates, and builds teams.
- The means by which work groups interface with employees in their units to imagine the possibilities for digital tools for their jobs.
- The foundation of the entire stage–gate process that builds a digital implementation plan.
- The medium by which the chairman facilitates, arbitrates, and coaches the steering committee.

We would actually go so far as to conclude that a digital undertaking in an organization *IS* the conversation about it.

### Element 7: Support

Chapter 4 dealt extensively with Support in an organization including the manager's responsibility for creating it and the employee's role in securing it. We illustrated in Figure 4.1 that healthy Support begins when conversations among managers and employees shift into dialogues and listening is empathic; greatest Support is achieved with presencing conversations and generative listening. We believe that during a digital undertaking (and all other times too) employees in an organization must be engaged in a conversation with someone, preferably their manager, about learning and performance. And we will repeat as we have stated before in this book that, "An organization will achieve its highest future potential when the employees feel that they will do the same."

Support is an imperative because it is the means by which talent is developed and retained in an organization. There is considerable research that demonstrates employee engagement is at its highest levels when employees are challenged to develop new skills and they believe that their contributions are valued.[40]

There is a fascinating consequence from implementing digital undertakings that is not entirely unexpected. It is commonly referred to as "taking the robot out of the human."[41] Digital tools unshackle employees from repetitive and routine tasks, enabling them to focus on more complex and higher-value work. Thus, at the core of digital transformations is talent development, i.e., providing employees with learning experiences and new growth opportunities.

It is called *digital upskilling* and it is a matter of viability in today's job market as digital technology redefines the way people work. It involves training that Millennial and Gen Z employees demand and what older employees need.[24] Formal training is just part of the learning need; it also involves stretch assignments, job shadowing, collaboration platforms, pop-up classes, innovation fellowships, peer-to-peer mentoring, learning hours, and reading clubs.[28]

Careers are either accelerated by newly learned digital skills or left behind if stagnant. This applies to employees and executives as well. Without constantly updated digital literacy at executive levels, an organization will become FUC'ed as it fails to keep abreast of emerging digital constraints and opportunities.

Support comes in forms other than upskilling; coaching is one that we have mentioned often throughout this chapter. During digital undertakings leaders often need to coach team members about deteriorating behaviors as they face conversion to new digital tools; the chairman may need to coach steering committee members to compromise their self-interests and allocate resources to digital investments that are best for the overall organization; and, the DIT Leader has a special role in coaching members in the organization as they progress through the challenges of becoming digitally mature.

## Element 8: Boundaries

We highlighted boundaries during the discussion of the Digital Initiative Team. For this section, however, we want to focus on inclusion. Specifically, who gets selected for the Digital Workgroups and the upskilling we just discussed above.

Even when demographic and cognitive diversity is fully embraced, and the other skill requirements are met (see section above for DIT Work Groups), there is always a temptation to include those who are thought to have the greatest headroom for growth, especially if they have demonstrated a disposition for digital technology. Therein lies a trap as this approach will result in the exclusion of large portions of the workforce with poor dispositions about digital technology, and perceptions of limited potential. This creates a major roadblock for successfully implementing a digital undertaking.

Inclusion is an essential boundary in order to ensure that all employees are part of a digital transformation. In Chapter 4 we mentioned our colleague Patty Beach and her concept of SHUVA. Organizations need *Digital SHUVA* where all employees feel *seen, heard, understood, valued, and appreciated* in a digitally maturing organization.

How do we achieve this? First, the conversational framework described for Support must be in place. Then employees must be put in a position that stimulates the development of digital-related skills – this could be a training program, for example. In inclusion theory, this is referred to as *positive position*, and any of the upskilling techniques described above can affect *positive position*.[42] A *positive position* with regard to digital technology will shape a *positive disposition* towards it, meaning being seen as having the confidence, determination, and commitment to take on new digital challenges. Notice that being given the opportunity to learn is what drives the willingness to learn.

Instead of picking people who have the perceived headroom for digital initiatives, build the headroom in all employees to achieve their fullest potential in a digitally maturing organization. The viability of a digital undertaking is heavily dependent on getting a critical mass of diverse employee in *positive digital positions*.

## Element 9: Space to Deliver

We noted in the discussion about data fatigue that leaders must provide the workforce with, among other things, the freedom and flexibility to use the digital tools and data effectively and experiment with new ideas while taking managed risks. Members of Digital Work Groups also must be given the space to participate in the digital initiative while maintaining their full-time positions.

More fundamentally, however, our prescription for *space to deliver* digital undertakings is the same as leadership in general – step back (but not away) and let employees deliver. Leaders shift their attention from the work of delivery onto the work of people by constantly focusing on future constraints and possibilities, fracturing ice, managing behavior, having conversations, shaping messages, monitoring performance, and providing support to people and the organization.

## FINAL WORDS

It is probably true that our brains have been altered by the effects of digital technology. Behind the scenes, digital technology has been impacting people and businesses over the last decade but for most of us the awareness of its disruptive and innovative nature is a recent phenomenon.

*Born-digital enterprises* clearly have a leg up on those *traditional enterprises* trying to adapt in a digital world. Maturing digitally involves reorganizing *external interfaces* and *internal structures and processes* to meet the expectations of customers, employees, and stakeholders who are increasingly connected to everything through social media, mobile devices, and the internet. In some cases it leads to new business models and entirely new businesses.

There is a mixed bag of successes and failures with digital undertakings. Common pitfalls result in stumbles for *traditional enterprises* as they try to remain competitive. We have illustrated in this chapter that NELM provides an excellent framework for success in an organization's digital undertaking. Creating and sustaining a viable *digital direction* is clearly the biggest challenge and it is also the key success factor. Building teams, setting boundaries, and creating a structure are equally critical and we outlined a Digital Initiative Team structure that greatly enhances the probability of a successful digital undertaking.

Once the direction, structure, boundaries, and teams are in place, a leader's attention turns to the assurance of enabling processes, behaviors, and conversations. Finally, the durability of the digital undertaking and ultimately the maturing of an organization are nurtured through support and creating the space to deliver.

## References

1 Prensky, M. (2001). Digital natives, digital immigrants. *On the Horizon*, 9(5). Retrieved April 4, 2021 from https://marcprensky.com/writing/Prensky%20 -%20Digital%20Natives,%20Digital%20Immigrants%20-%20Part1.pdf.

2  Albright, J. (2019). *Left to their own devices: How digital natives are reshaping the American dream*. New York, NY: Prometheus.

3  Gartner.com (n.d.). 10 management techniques from born-digital companies. Retrieved April 4, 2021 from www.gartner.com/smarterwithgartner/ 10-management-techniques-from-born-digital-companies/.

4  Encyclopedia.com (n.d.). Digital technology. Retrieved March 15, 2021 www.encyclopedia.com/history/dictionaries-thesauruses-pictures-and-press-releases/ digital-technology.

5  Shannon, CE., & Weaver, W. (1963). *The mathematical theory of communication* (4th ed.). Urbana, IL: University of Illinois Press, p. 144.

6  IBM Cloud Education (2020, June 3). Artificial intelligence (AI). Retrieved March 15, 2021 from www.ibm.com/cloud/learn/what-is-artificial-intelligence.

7  Azure Digital Twins (n.d.). Retrieved March 16, 2021 from https://azure. microsoft.com/en-us/resources/videos/azure-digital-twins-video/.

8  Daugherty, P., Carrel-Billiard, M., & Biltz, M. (n.d.). Every leader is a technology leader: Embracing a new mindset to shape a better future. Accenture: Technology Vision 21. Retrieved March 16, 2021 from www.accenture.com/ us-en/insights/technology/technology-trends-2021?c=acn_glb_technolog yvisiobing_12046542&n=psbs_0321&msclkid=44a6297120ad134afee4493 ddedc284a&utm_source=bing&utm_medium=cpc&utm_campaign=US_ EXPT_CORP_NA_TECHVIZ_GENERIC_EXCT_STND_EN_NA_ SRVC-TECHENT-TECHINNOENT-NA_NA_General&utm_term=digital%20 technology&utm_content=CONS_ENT_NA_TECHVIZ_NA_SRVC-TECHENT-TECHINNOENT-NA_NA_Digital%20Technology.

9  Boag, P. (2014, August 19). Definition of digital: What the heck is 'digital' anyway? *Boagworld*. Retrieved March 15, 2021 from https://boagworld.com/audio/ definition-digital/.

10  Fitzgerald, M., Kruschwitz, N., Bonnet, D., & Welsh, M. (2013). Embracing digital technology: A new strategic imperative. *MIT Sloan Management Review*. Retrieved from https://sloanreview.mit.edu/projects/embracing-digital-technology/.

11  Ward, L. (2021, March 27). Can artificial intelligence replace human therapists? *Wall Street Journal*. Retrieved March 30, 2021 from www.wsj.com/articles/ can-artificial-intelligence-replace-human-therapists-11616857200.

12  Kane, G. C., Palmer, D., Phillips, A. N., Kiron, D., & Buckley, N. (2016, July 26). Aligning the organization for its digital future. *MIT Sloan Management Review*. Retrieved April 5, 2021 from https://sloanreview.mit.edu/projects/ aligning-for-digital-future/.

13  Reeves, M., Levin, S., & Ueda, D. (2016). The biology of corporate survival. *Harvard Business Review*. Retrieved April 5, 2021 from https://hbr.org/2016/01/ the-biology-of-corporate-survival.

14  Top companies for innovation. (2021). *Wall Street Journal*. Retrieved April 5, 2021 from www.wsj.com/articles/top-companies-for-innovation-11615931461.

15  Morgan, G. (2019, November 12). Suncor deal with Microsoft for digital transformation first for the oilsands. *Financial Post*. Retrieved April 5, 20221 from https:// financialpost.com/commodities/energy/suncor-strikes-deal-with-microsoft-for-digital-transformation-in-first-for-the-oilsands#:~:text=Suncor%20deal%20 with%20Microsoft%20for%20digital%20transformation%20first,of%20cloud%20 computing%2C%20artificial%20intelligence%20and%20machine%20learning.

16  Adamczyk, D. (n.d.). Thriving in the digital era. Leadership in Action. Retrieved April 5, 2021 from https://partners.wsj.com/ey/leadership-in-action/thriving-in-the-digital-era/.

17  Mann, T., & Gryta, T. (2020, July 18). The dimming of GE's bold digital dreams. *Wall Street Journal*. Retrieved April 6, 2021 from www.wsj.com/articles/the-dimming-of-ges-bold-digital-dreams-11595044802.

18  April, K., and Dalwai, A. (2019). Leadership styles required to lead digital transformation. *Effective Executive, XXII*(2), 14–45.

19  Kurt Lewin's change management model: The planned approach to organizational change. (n.d.). *MSG*. Retrieved May 28, 2021 from www.managementstudyguide.com/kurt-lewins-change-management-model.htm.

20  Leonardi, P. (2019, December 10). You're going digital: Now what? *MIT Sloan Review*. Retrieved April 8, 2021 from https://sloanreview.mit.edu/article/youre-going-digital-now-what/.

21  Senge, P. M. (1997). Communities of leaders and learners. *Harvard Business Review*, 75(5), September/October, 30–32.

22  Gale, M., & Aarons, C. (2018). Digital transformation. *Leader to Leader*, (Fall), 30–35.

23  Digitaldefynd. (n.d.). 10 best digital transformation courses and certification. Retrieved May 28, 2021 from https://digitaldefynd.com/best-digital-transformation-courses/#1_Digital_Transformation_MIT_Professional_Education.

24  Clark, S. (2020, January 31). Optimizing your company's culture for today's modern workers. *CMS Wire*. Retrieved April 9, 2021 from www.cmswire.com/digital-workplace/optimizing-your-company-culture-for-the-todays-modern-workers/.

25  Mimms, C. (2021, April 10). As Apple and Facebook clash over ads, mom-and-pop shops fear that they'll be the victims. *Wall Street Journal*. Retrieved on April 11, 2021 from www.wsj.com/articles/apple-facebook-clash-over-ads-small-businesses-fear-theyll-be-impacted-11618009627.

26  Bughin, J., Deakin, J., & O'Beirne, B. (2019). Digital transformation: Improving the odds of success. *The McKinsey Quarterly*, October 22. Retrieved from www.mckinsey.com/~/media/McKinsey/Business%20Functions/McKinsey%20Digital/Our%20Insights/Digital%20transformation%20Improving%20the%20odds%20of%20success/Digital-transformation-Improving-the-odds-of-success-final.pdf#:~:text=Digital%20transformation%3A%20Improving%20the%20odds%20of%20success%20Most,by%20Jacques%20Bughin%2C%20Jonathan%20Deakin%2C%20and%20Barbara%20O%E2%80%99Beirne.

27  Ibarra, H. (2020). Take a wrecking ball to your company's iconic practices. *MIT Sloan Management Review*, Winter. Retrieved from https://sloanreview.mit.edu/article/take-a-wrecking-ball-to-your-companys-iconic-practices/.

28  Westerman, G., Soule, D., & Eswaran, A. (2019). Building digital-ready culture in traditional organizations. *MIT Sloan Management Review*, Summer. Retrieved from https://sloanreview.mit.edu/article/building-digital-ready-culture-in-traditional-organizations/.

29  Kane, G., Palmer, D., Phillips, A., Kiron, D., & Buckley, N. (2016). Aligning the organization for its digital future. *MIT Sloan Management Review*, Deloitte University Press, July. Retrieved from https://sloanreview.mit.edu/projects/aligning-for-digital-future/.

30  Kane, G., Nguyen Philips, A., Copulsky, J., & Andrus, G. (2019). How digital leadership is(n't) different. *MIT Sloan Management Review*, Spring. Retrieved from https://sloanreview.mit.edu/article/how-digital-leadership-isnt-different/.

31  Fitzgerald, M., Kruschwitz, N., Bonnet, D., & Welch, M. (2013). Embracing digital technology. *MIT Sloan Management Review*, Capgemini Consulting. Retrieved from https://sloanreview.mit.edu/projects/embracing-digital-technology/.

32 McKinsey Digital. (2019, April 24). Five moves to make during a digital transformation. Retrieved May 4, 2021 from www.mckinsey.com/business-functions/mckinsey-digital/our-insights/five-moves-to-make-during-a-digital-transformation.

33 Matt, C., Hess, T., & Benlian, A. (2015). Digital transformation strategies. *Business & Information Systems Engineering, 57*(5), 339–343.

34 Slot, O. (2018). *The talent lab.* London: Penguin Random House.

35 Stratton, R. W. (2003). Project gates: "Chutes and Ladders®" for project managers. Paper presented at PMI® Global Congress 2003 – EMEA, The Hague, South Holland, The Netherlands. Newtown Square, PA: Project Management Institute. Retrieved May 5, 2021 from www.pmi.org/learning/library/contemporary-gate-philosophy-implemented-outcome-7786.

36 Cross, R., Edmondson, A., & Murphy, W. (2020). A noble purpose alone won't transform your company. *MIT Sloan Management Review.* Retrieved from https://sloanreview.mit.edu/article/a-noble-purpose-alone-wont-transform-your-company/.

37 Mickle, T. (2021, May 11). Google plans to double AI ethics research staff. *Wall Street Journal.* Retrieved May 11, 2021 from www.wsj.com/articles/google-plans-to-double-ai-ethics-research-staff-11620749048.

38 Ward, L. (2021, March 27). Can artificial intelligence replace human therapists? *Wall Street Journal.* Retrieved May 14, 2021 from www.wsj.com/articles/can-artificial-intelligence-replace-human-therapists-11616857200.

39 Weick, K., (1995) *Sensemaking in organizations.* Thousand Oaks, CA: SAGE Publications

40 Saks, A. (2019). Antecedents and consequences of employee engagement revisited. *Journal of Organizational Effectiveness: People and Performance, 6*(1), 19–38.

41 Barton, K. (n.d.). How law departments can learn from tax and finance transformations. *Wall Street Journal.* Retrieved May 15, 2021 from https://partners.wsj.com/ey/the-shift/how-law-departments-can-learn-from-tax-and-finance-transformations/.

42 Hyter, M. C., Turnock, J. L., & Kilts, J. M. (2009) *The power of inclusion: Unlock the potential and productivity of your workforce.* Hoboken, NJ: Wiley.

# CONCLUDING THOUGHTS

We wrote this book as a compendium of topics for use with our first two books, *Applied Leadership Development*, and its revision *Becoming a Leader*. Our purpose was to illustrate how leadership, especially our NELM model, applies to nearly all situations that people and organizations will confront. We also wanted to demonstrate the veracity of our thesis that, "the root cause of everything that goes right or wrong in an organization is leadership, be that human or divine."

We tested the thesis against an amazingly broad range of challenges, situations, and beliefs: godliness, Machiavellianism, making good decisions, media bias and bias in general, meaning of time, confronting life's challenges and constraints, COVID-19 pandemic, understanding stress, supporting people to become the best version of themselves, helping oneself through a career crisis, resilience, listening generously, building healthy relationships, hugging people psychologically, creating a healthy culture imbued with dignity and respect, diversity quotas, workplace toxicity, creating an equitable and inclusive workplace, and achieving and sustaining organizational viability in a digital world.

Along the way we stumbled across confirmation of our belief that everything in life results from relationships. By asking a colleague to review a draft of our chapter "Breaking the 4th Wall," our leadership behavior guidelines were seen by a group of real estate attorneys in Texas, and through a random connection of relationships, the guidelines were chosen as the basis for an "Equality Pledge" by Community Associations Institute (CAI), an international organization with over 40,000 members. We are proud to be a part of CAI's journey of building better communities worldwide – those that promote togetherness, neighborliness, belonging, and connection. To view the pledge see **www.caionline.org/HomeownerLeaders/Documents/CAIDiverse CommunitiesGuide041521.pdf**.

We are also proud of our relationship with you, our readers. You honor us by purchasing and reading our books and we hope that they make a positive difference as you deepen your journey through life.

Al and Leanne

# INDEX

Locators in *italics* refer to figures.

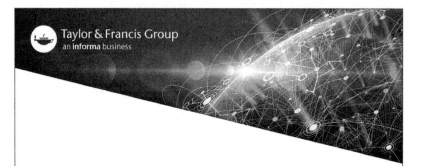

Printed in the United States
by Baker & Taylor Publisher Services